BLOCK 3   VOLCANIC ARCS

Prepared by Steve Blake for the Course Team

CONTENTS

The S339 Course Team

Chairman
Richard Thorpe

Course Manager
Val Russell

Authors
Steve Blake
Geoff Brown
Rob Butler
Steve Drury
Nigel Harris
Chris Hawkesworth
Richard Thorpe

Editors
Gerry Bearman
David Tillotson

Designer
Sarah Powell

Graphic Artists
Sue Dobson
Ray Munns

BBC
Andrew Crilly
David Jackson
Nick Watson

The Open University
Walton Hall, Milton Keynes
MK7 6AA

First published 1990

Designed by the Graphic Design Group of the Open University.

Typeset and printed in Great Britain by Henry Ling Ltd, The Dorset Press, Dorchester, Dorset.

ISBN 0 7492 5021 6

This Block forms part of an Open University course: S339 Understanding the Continents. The complete list of Blocks is on the back cover. If you have not enrolled on the course and would like to buy this or other Open University material, please write to Open University Educational Enterprises Ltd, 12 Cofferidge Close, Stony Stratford, MK11 1BY, Great Britain. If you wish to enquire about enrolling as an Open University student, please write to The Admissions Office, The Open University, PO Box 48, Walton Hall, Milton Keynes, MK7 6AB, Great Britain.

1.1

Table A   Scientific terms and concepts introduced or developed in Block 3

OBJECTIVES FOR BLOCK 3

When you have completed this Block, you should be able to:

1   Define and use, or recognize correct definitions and applications of, each of the terms listed in Table A.

2   Account for subduction zone magmatism in terms of the P-T conditions, chemical composition and phase diagrams of relevant source material and primary magmas.

3   Use observed subduction zone parameters to support or challenge various hypotheses of magma generation in subduction zones.

4   Recognize tholeiitic and calc-alkaline trends on FeO_t/MgO versus SiO_2 and AFM (alkalis–FeO_t–MgO) diagrams.

5   Use the chemical composition of a lava from a subduction zone volcano to classify it using the appropriate diagrams (K_2O versus SiO_2, FeO_t/MgO versus SiO_2, AFM).

6   Describe and account for correlations between magma composition and the Mg content (and Mg ratio) of ferromagnesian minerals and An content of plagioclase in equilibrium with those magmas.

7   Complete simple calculations using the Rayleigh fractionation equation.

8   Plot appropriate chemical data on log–log graph paper, and assess whether or not the resultant trend may have arisen through fractional crystallization.

9   Determine the bulk partition coefficient of a compatible trace element from an appropriate log–log variation diagram.

10   Complete simple calculations to relate the bulk partition coefficient of a compatible trace element to the likely mineralogy of the fractionating assemblage.

11   Use rare earth element (REE) patterns to discuss the fractionation history of a magma, particularly the relative importance of plagioclase fractionation or accumulation.

12   Plot an appropriate variation diagram to distinguish mixed magmas from those of a fractionated series.

13   Given the mineralogy, mineral compositions and textures in an igneous rock, suggest whether or not that rock was formed by magma mixing.

14   Describe the density relations among the magmas of a fractionated calc-alkaline magma series, and use this to account for compositionally zoned magma chambers.

15   Give an account of the volcanic history and magmatic processes associated with Santorini.

16   Describe the major differences in the crustal structures and magma compositions found at island arcs and at active continental margins.

17   Give a brief account of the crustal thickness, basement geology, volcanology and slab geometry along the Andean plate boundary.

18   Perform simple graphical tests of geochemical data to assess the role of crustal contamination in the evolution of a magma series and relate your conclusions to possible mechanisms of contamination (assimilation with fractional crystallization (AFC), thermal erosion).

19   Outline the physical circumstances under which magma can be contaminated by crustal rocks.

20   Use the quartz–alkali feldspar–plagioclase (QAP) diagram to classify granitoids.

21   Outline the geochemistry of plutonic rocks from subduction zones.

22   Relate the plutonic geology of South American batholiths to processes of crustal growth and subduction.

23   Relate episodes of terrane accretion and arc magmatism to the geometry of plate convergence.

24 Discuss the extent to which subduction zone processes have contributed to crustal growth rates throughout Earth history.

25 Outline evidence for subduction zone processes in the British geological record.

26 Discuss the interpretation of this evidence in terms of large-scale plate margin processes.

1 INTRODUCTION AND STUDY COMMENT

Subduction zones (Figure 1.1) occur at destructive plate margins, where dense oceanic lithosphere descends into the mantle. New crust is generated by the emplacement of magmas at subduction zones, while sedimentation, metamorphism and tectonism rearrange the pre-existing geology there. Our general understanding of

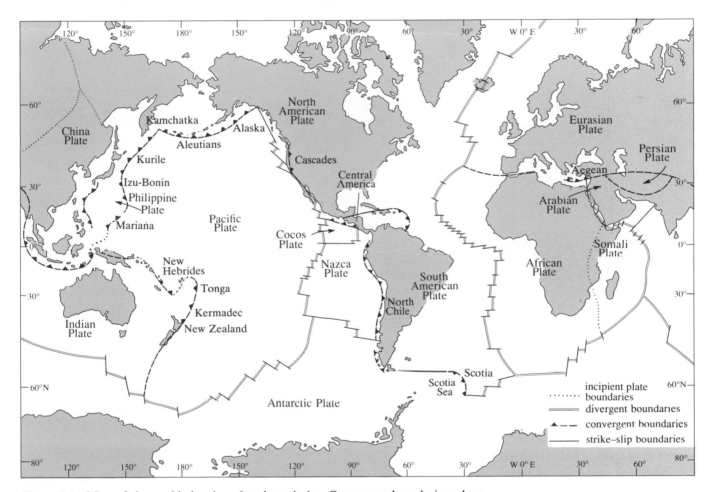

Figure 1.1 Map of the world showing plate boundaries. Convergent boundaries where oceanic lithosphere is being subducted (destructive plate margins) are shown by teeth.

subduction processes has come from a combination of geophysical and geological observations. These background results, which will be familiar to you from earlier courses, are summarized in Figure 1.2.

Earthquakes occur where the cold upper part of the sinking oceanic lithosphere experiences volume changes and generates mechanical friction against the overriding crust and mantle (Figure 1.2a). The position of the slab, or descending plate, is thus identified by this region of earthquakes, known as the Benioff zone, which in some cases is found extending to depths of 700 km. Magmatism at subduction zones occurs in a narrow volcanic arc above the Benioff zone and parallel to the plate boundary. The magmas are commonly andesitic in composition and contain several percent dissolved water, but at low pressures this exsolves to fuel highly explosive eruptions, making subduction zone volcanoes the world's most dangerous.

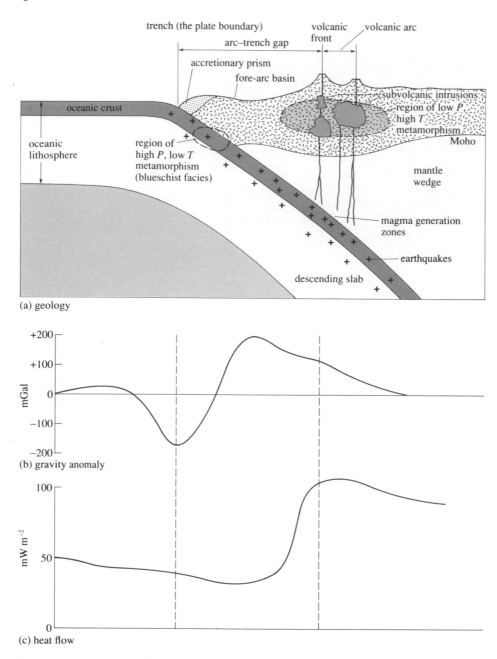

(a) geology

(b) gravity anomaly

(c) heat flow

Figure 1.2 Schematic diagrams of the geological and selected geophysical features of subduction zones taken perpendicular to the plate boundary. (a) Cross section through a destructive plate margin identifying the major geological features and terminology. (b) Sketch of the gravity anomaly measured across a destructive plate margin. (c) Sketch of the surface heat flow measured across a destructive plate margin.

Destructive plate boundaries are defined by the deep trenches where ocean lithosphere starts to subduct. These are the topographically lowest regions of the Earth's surface, with some trenches bottoming out 11 km below sea-level. The topographic expression around subduction zones is striking, especially close to western South America where the Peru–Chile trench (depth 7 km) lies within 600 km of the crest of the Andes, where summits above 6 km are common. Many trenches are partly filled with sediment scraped from the top of the descending ocean plate or washed in from the overriding plate. Over time, the rich supply of sediment results in an accretionary prism many tens of kilometres wide and several kilometres thick.

The geophysical expression of the trench is clear in the gravity measurements (Figure 1.2b), with the deep water-filled depression giving rise to a large negative gravity anomaly. In contrast, a positive gravity anomaly above much of the forearc reflects the high density of the underlying slab.

Heat flow measurements also vary across subduction zones (Figures 1.2c and Block 1A, Figure 2.17). In the forearc region, surface heat flow is low due to the cold oceanic lithosphere beneath this area. Metamorphism in the deeper parts of the forearc thus take place at high pressure and (compared with normal geotherms) low temperature. These conditions produce glaucophane and lawsonite-bearing metamorphic assemblages, and you may recall the term glaucophane–lawsonite facies, which has been used to identify them. Because glaucophane, a blue amphibole, is commonly developed in the metasediments and metabasalts around subduction zones, an equivalent name is the blueschist facies. This contrasts with the greenschist and amphibolite facies metamorphism of the volcanic arc crust, where, because of magmatic activity, the heat flow is high (Figure 1.2c) such that metamorphism takes place in conditions of low pressure and high temperature (Figure 1.2a).

All of the above subduction processes rely on the ocean lithosphere moving directly towards and beneath the overriding plate. You will know from Block 1A, however, that oblique subduction is common and leads to transpression. The resultant strike–slip motion at destructive plate boundaries causes the dislocation, transport and docking of terranes (Block 1A, Section 3.3). In this Block, we shall come across some of the effects of terrane movement.

In Section 2, we examine the processes that generate primary magmas at subduction zones and so initiate crustal growth. Sections 3 and 4 amplify certain parts of Block 2 by further developing techniques with which to interpret geochemical and petrographic observations in terms of magmatic processes. These reveal the importance of crustal structure on magmatic processes by contrasting the evolution of magmas at subduction zones where the crust is thin (the Aegean arc, see Figure 1.1) or thick (the Andes). Having gained an appreciation for present-day, observable, processes, Section 5 considers the geology of the eroded volcanic arcs, batholiths and terrane boundaries of South America. Even older subduction zone rocks are found in Britain, and these are studied in Section 6.

Throughout the Block, we refer to material in the Colour Plate Booklet (CPB) and to features and localities seen on the Tectonic Map of the Earth (TMOE), so you will need these to hand. Block 3 also has one video programme associated with it, VC 272: *Island Arc Magmatism: Santorini*, which you should view at the point indicated in the text (Section 3). And there is a home kit exercise relating to some igneous rocks emplaced within the Southern Uplands during Caledonian subduction. You will be directed to this exercise at the appropriate point in Section 6; this Section also requires you to have the Tay Forth geological map to hand.

2 ORIGIN OF MAGMATISM AT SUBDUCTION ZONES

One of the most obvious questions to ask about subduction zones is 'why are subduction zones characterized by magmatic activity?' Attempts to answer this have often been concerned with explaining why andesites are the typical magma composition. However, basalts, which are more primitive, are found in volcanic arcs too, and are seen to be parental to the andesites. A more pertinent question then is 'what is the origin of basalt magmas at subduction zones?' Various explanations have been proposed which rely on one or other of the following three mechanisms:

Mechanism 1—Frictional heating Friction between the upper surface of the slab and the overriding mantle wedge may cause the contact zone to melt.

Mechanism 2—Melting of the slab As the slab descends into the mantle, it heats up. If the temperature becomes sufficiently high, then the slab, and in particular its more fusible parts—the upper layers of sediment and hydrothermally altered basalt, may undergo partial melting to generate magmas.

Mechanism 3—Melting of the wedge As the slab descends, it undergoes metamorphic reactions involving the dehydration of hydrous minerals (such as clays, chlorite and amphiboles). If the released water then migrates up into the mantle wedge, partial melting can occur, to produce basalt. This mechanism relies on the fact that the melting temperature (solidus) of wet mantle peridotite is lower than that of normal, dry peridotite. ✗

As with many geological problems, assessing which of these three mechanisms is most likely rests on a careful examination of geological observations together with the findings of controlled laboratory experiments or theoretical predictions. For example, some people have tried to calculate or reproduce the pressure and temperature conditions within the Benioff zone in order to predict where melting might occur. Others have been guided by what can be observed at the surface.

> If frictional heating was the cause of arc magmatism, would you expect the distance between the volcanic arc and the trench to correlate with the rate of subduction?

A rapidly subducting slab would generate heat rapidly and so volcanism would be expected relatively close to the trench. According to this idea, a plot of the arc-to-trench distance against subduction rate should show a negative slope. Data from many subduction zones are plotted in Figure 2.1. The convergence rates of oceanic lithosphere towards a subduction zone range from less than 1 cm a^{-1} up to 12 cm a^{-1}. Arc-trench distances range from 100 km to almost 500 km, but do not correlate with convergence rate (Figure 2.1). We have to conclude, therefore, that frictional heating plays little or no role in the generation of arc magmas.

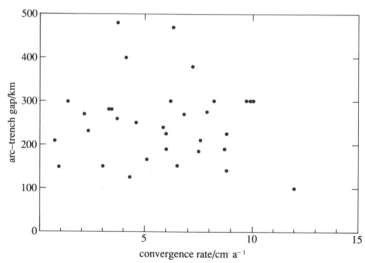

Figure 2.1   Distance from the trench to the volcanic front (the arc–trench gap of Figure 1.2a) plotted against the speed of the subducting slab.

To decide between melting of the slab (mechanism 2) and melting of the mantle wedge (mechanism 3), we can recall that the composition of a magma's source rock has some bearing on the composition of the magma. During partial melting, the minerals with low melting points are first to melt so that the partial melt is more siliceous than the source rock. Thus, the basaltic part of the slab can yield andesitic partial melts, whilst the peridotite in the mantle wedge will yield basaltic partial melts. Laboratory experiments have confirmed that this is the case, demonstrating that the basaltic primary magmas do not come from the slab but from within the mantle wedge. It then remains to discover why melting of the mantle should be linked to subduction of oceanic lithosphere.

The behaviour of the subducted ocean crust as pressure (P) and temperature (T) increase with depth in the subduction zone is important here, and can be illustrated using the phase diagram in Figure 2.2a. This diagram also shows two P–T paths, which geophysicists have suggested as possible descriptions of the heating experienced by the descending ocean crust. For the time being, we shall concentrate on the upper curve, and the marked points 'a', 'b' and 'c', which correspond to the locations marked in the cartoon subduction zone of Figure 2.2b.

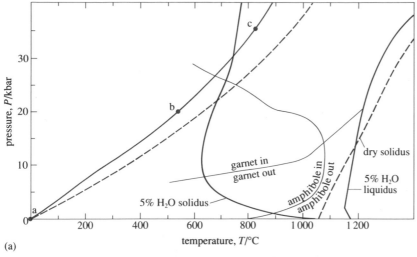

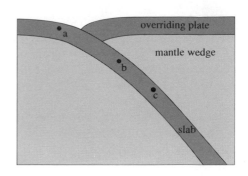

(a) (b)

Figure 2.2 (a) *P–T* diagram showing the solidus and the stability limits of amphibole and garnet in basalt containing 5% water, and the solidus of anhydrous basalt. Pyroxene is present at all temperatures, except near the rocks' liquidus temperatures. The hydrous basalt composition is representative of altered ocean crust. The *P–T* paths, in red, indicate conditions experienced by the oceanic crust as it descends into the mantle at a subduction zone. (b)   Sketch of the subducting slab, mantle wedge and overriding plate indicating the positions of the points 'a', 'b' and 'c' appearing in Figure 2.2a.

At point 'a' in Figure 2.2b, the ocean crust comprises mainly altered basalt containing about 3 to 5% water bound up in clay minerals and chlorite. As these rocks are subducted and evolve along the geotherm of Figure 2.2a, they undergo a series of metamorphic reactions. By the time the slab has reached point 'b' at 60 km depth (pressure of *c*.20 kbar) the ocean crust has been metamorphosed to amphibolite, a rock comprising amphibole, garnet and pyroxene.

What happens on moving to greater depth, say point 'c'?

With increasing *P* and *T*, the rock crosses out of the stability field of amphibole. This takes place at between 25 and 30 kbar.

At all higher pressures, anhydrous eclogite consisting just of garnet, pyroxene and a silica polymorph, is stable, together with water vapour or fluid. This fluid is mobile and free to escape from the slab, and because of its low density rises into the mantle wedge leaving dry eclogite behind. Now, eclogite (3.4×10^3 kg m^{-3}) is denser than either amphibolite (3.0×10^3 kg m^{-3}) or mantle peridotite (3.3×10^3 kg m^{-3}), so the amphibolite to eclogite transition increases the average density of the slab and helps it to sink further into the mantle.

At point 'c', the slab is anhydrous and at a temperature several hundred degrees below its solidus. Thus the slab cannot undergo partial melting once it has been dehydrated by the reaction

$$amphibolite \rightarrow eclogite + water$$

This having been said, however, some geophysicists have made other computer calculations of geotherms that cross the solidus of wet basalt before moving out of the amphibole stability field. The lower geotherm on Figure 2.2a is an example of one such geotherm. However, we have already argued that partial melting of the slab cannot explain the origin of *basalt* in volcanic arcs, so the geological evidence indicates that low geothermal gradients are untenable or that less hydrous basalt, with higher solidus temperatures, characterizes subducted oceanic crust. Certainly 5% water is a maximum for the rocks on the sea floor, so the solidus shown in Figure 2.2a probably underestimates the temperature required to melt the slab. More realistic values may be a hundred degrees or so higher.

This leaves us to contemplate the mantle wedge. Just as the solidus temperature of the slab is increased when it dehydrates, so the solidus temperature of mantle peridotite will be lowered on receiving water from the slab. Arguments abound as to

10

whether this wet mantle will be sufficiently wet or sufficiently hot to undergo partial melting next to the Benioff zone. None the less, it is certain that the addition of water to the mantle will lower its density and allow diapirs of hot, wet, peridotite to rise through the mantle wedge (Figure 2.3).

As you learned in Block 1A (Section 2.1.1), the adiabatic rise of peridotite leads to partial melting and the generation of basalt magma. Following this reasoning, we can predict that basalt will be generated as wet mantle diapirs rise through the mantle wedge. These magmas would then be ultimately erupted in the volcanic arc (Figure 2.3).

Can you think of a way to test this link between slab dehydration, mantle diapirs and arc volcanism?

In the model of arc magmagenesis (i.e. arc petrogenesis), a key feature is the dehydration reaction.

$$amphibolite \rightarrow eclogite + water$$

which according to Figure 2.2a, occurs at around 25 to 30 kbar, the exact pressure depending on the exact temperature and water content of the slab.

If this is indeed the trigger that initiates magma generation beneath volcanic arcs then the volcanoes should be directly above the site at which the slab dehydrates (as indicated in Figure 2.3). The depth to the top of the slab beneath a volcanic arc is found from the distribution of seismicity and allows us to compare the **volcano–slab depth, h**, with the depth at which we predict the slab to dehydrate.

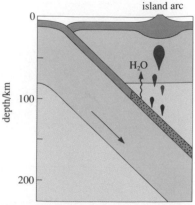

Figure 2.3 Cartoon of the processes occurring within a subduction zone that lead to the generation of parental basalt magma in the mantle wedge. Oceanic crust subducts containing 3 to 5% water but becomes dehydrated at a pressure of 25 to 30 kbar, driving the released water into the mantle wedge. The hydrated peridotite is light and rises, undergoing adiabatic decompression and subsequent partial melting. The basaltic liquids segregate out of the mantle diapirs and are added to the crust as plutons and volcanic rocks.

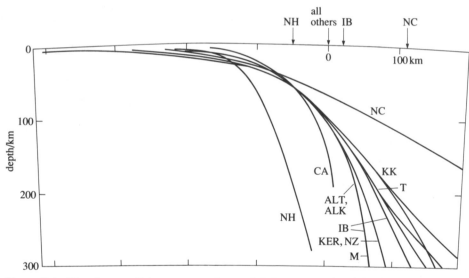

Figure 2.4 The shapes of the upper surfaces of slabs at several subduction zones, based on the distribution of earthquake foci. The subduction zones are: ALK (Alaska), ALT (Aleutians), CA (Central America), IB (Izu-Bonin), KER(Kermadec), KK (Kurile/Kamchatka), M (Mariana), NC (North Chile), NH (New Hebrides, also known as Vanuatu), NZ (New Zealand) and T (Tonga). Their locations can be found on Figure 1.1 (also see TMOE). Arrow heads show the position of the volcanic arcs. The curvature of the Earth's surface is shown.

ITQ 2.1 Estimate the depth, h, to the Benioff zone beneath the volcanic front at each of the subduction zones illustrated in Figure 2.4.

A fuller picture emerges when data from all of the world's subduction zones are considered. Thirty-one measurements are summarized in a histogram of h values in Figure 2.5.

Some volcanic arcs sit above deep Benioff zones ($h \approx 200$ km), but, as you found in answering ITQ 2.1, in most cases h is closer to 100 km. The exceptions occur where the slab subducts at an abnormally steep angle or very slow rate, but under normal circumstances, the average value of h is 112 km, with most subduction zones being

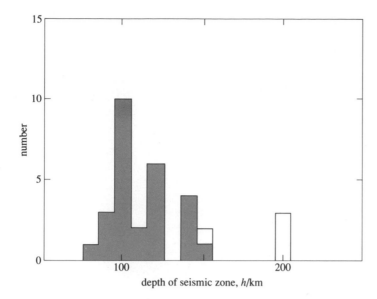

Figure 2.5 Histogram of the vertical distance (h) between the top of the Benioff zone and the volcanic front at 31 subduction sites. White areas indicate cases with unusually steep subduction angles ($>70°$) or unusually slow rates of subduction (<1 cm a^{-1}). In all other cases (grey), the subduction angle is between $30°$ and $70°$, and the subduction speed is between 1 and 12 cm a^{-1}.

within 20 km of this value. Usually, the volcanic front is situated from 90 to 130 km above the slab (Figure 2.5). Considering that we are dealing with a complex natural phenomenon, and that there is uncertainty of ±5 or 10 km in defining each value of h, this is a remarkably close clustering of measurements. This fits with our expectation of a pressure-sensitive mechanism within the slab which triggers arc magmatism.

> **ITQ 2.2** (a) What range of pressures characterize the top of the slab beneath most volcanic fronts? (Recall that pressure $P=\rho gh$, where ρ is the average density of the overlying rocks—assume a value of 3.3×10^{3} kg m^{-3} here—and g is the acceleration due to gravity $=10$ m s^{-2}. Note that 1 kg m^{-1} s$^{-2}=1$ Pa $=10^{-5}$ bar.)
>
> (b) Do the pressures calculated in (a) coincide with those at which the ocean crust is predicted to dehydrate?

Earthquakes within the slab beneath the volcanic front occur at slightly deeper levels than those at which amphibolite is expected to de-water. However, seismic activity is more likely in the cold brittle interior of the slab than in the warm outer regions, which include the amphibolite and eclogite of the metamorphosed oceanic crust. Taking this into account allows a more convincing match between the dehydration pressure and the seismic and volcanic activity. Thus the geological and geophysical observations come together with the arguments based on the geotherms and the phase diagram of Figure 2.2a in a consistent model of arc magmagenesis. The process starts with dehydration of the oceanic crust at depths of approximately 100 km (pressure around 25 to 30 kbar). The released water migrates into the mantle wedge, creating buoyant diapirs of wet peridotite that rise through the mantle wedge and experience adiabatic decompression and partial melting. The resultant basalt magmas enter the crust and erupt along the volcanic arc. Furthermore, certain volatile trace elements are believed to be carried into the mantle by hydrous fluid escaping from the slab. These elements may then account for the distinctive trace element signatures found in subduction zone basalts (Block 2, Figure 4.1).

Our general model of *basalt* petrogenesis cannot be the whole story of arc magmatism, however. As you know, more evolved magmas and in particular andesites are much more common in volcanic arcs. To understand the processes that allow this, the next two Sections of this Block concentrate on unravelling the magmatic processes that occur in the crust. In addition, we shall also consider how the crust itself

12

influences these processes. Volcanic arcs above subduction zones can rest on either thin, basic, ocean crust (i.e. island arcs such as Mariana, Tonga and Kermadec, Figure 1.1, TMOE) or thick, intermediate, continental crust (i.e. **active continental margins** such as the Andes, Figure 1.1, TMOE) providing us with a global natural laboratory in which to study interactions between crustal and magmatic processes in areas of crustal growth.

Summary

Various hypotheses of magma generation at subduction zones can be tested using a combination of geological, geophysical and laboratory evidence. Frictional heating between the slab and the mantle wedge is discounted as a mechanism for generating magmas because there is no correlation between the speed of subduction, and hence rate of heating, with the proximity of the volcanic front to the trench. Instead, the volcanic front is typically situated at a near-constant height, h, of 90 to 130 km above the Benioff zone indicating that a pressure-sensitive reaction in the slab triggers magma genesis. The possibility that magmas are formed by partial melting of sub-ducted ocean crust can be discounted on the basis that this process would produce andesites, whereas basalts are observed to be the most primitive arc magmas. The phase diagram of wet basalt, such as that forming subducted ocean crust, together with calculated P–T conditions along the interface between the Benioff zone and the mantle wedge indicates that the dehydration reaction amphibolite→eclogite+ water will take place in the pressure interval 25 to 30 kbar. This pressure-sensitive reaction supplies water, and possibly other volatile elements, to the mantle wedge. The resultant wet peridotite rises because of its buoyancy, undergoing adiabatic decompression and partial melting to produce basalt. The volcanic front is thus situated directly above the site of slab dehydration.

SAQS FOR SECTION 2

SAQ 2.1 Describe whether each of the following statements is true or false.

(a) Andesite is most probably the primary magma at subduction zone volcanoes.

(b) Basalt in the oceanic lithosphere is dry (anhydrous) when it is subducted.

(c) The uppermost part of the slab beneath volcanic arcs is typically at a pressure of 30 to 43 kbar.

(d) At a given pressure, the solidus temperature of dry basalt is lower than that of wet (hydrous) basalt.

(e) At pressures close to 25 kbar, the amphibolite to eclogite reaction can take place only within a very small range of temperatures.

(f) In most subduction zones, one of the products of the amphibolite to eclogite reaction is a silicate melt (magma).

SAQ 2.2 What are the anticipated compositions of partial melts of (a) the subducted slab and (b) the mantle wedge?

SAQ 2.3 Which observed parameters can be used to test the frictional heating model of arc magma genesis?

SAQ 2.4 Under what circumstances could slab-melting be a viable mechanism for generating magmas at subduction zones? What is the major piece of evidence that suggests partial melting of the slab is not primarily responsible for arc magmas?

3 MAGMAS AND MAGMATIC PROCESSES AT AN ISLAND ARC VOLCANO: SANTORINI

One of the world's most thoroughly studied subduction zone volcanoes is found in Europe. This is Santorini, which is one of the volcanic centres that define the Aegean arc, in the Mediterranean Sea (Figure 3.1). Here, we shall examine the geology and geochemistry of the Santorini volcano in order to develop and apply a number of techniques for interpreting igneous processes. We shall thus discover specific points about a subduction zone volcano, whilst learning some general principles that are routinely applied to suites of volcanic rocks in order to understand the workings of sub-volcanic magma systems.

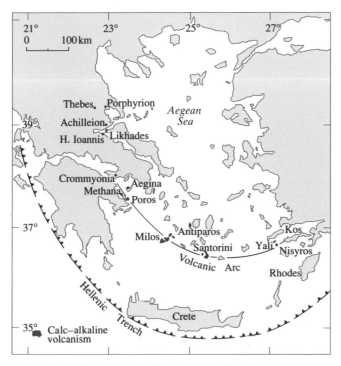

Figure 3.1 Map showing the location of volcanoes within the Aegean arc, north of the Hellenic Trench.

3.1 REGIONAL SETTING AND HISTORY OF THE AEGEAN ARC

The Aegean arc lies about 250 km north of the Hellenic trench system where the African Plate starts to descend beneath the Eurasian Plate (TMOE, Figures 1.1, 3.1). The trench marks the southern edge of the Aegean microplate, which is interpreted to abut the Eurasian Plate proper along transform faults in northern Greece and Turkey. One of these is the Anatolian Fault, which is shown on TMOE. The Aegean microplate has thin (20–30 km) continental-type crust. Earthquake foci define a Benioff zone, which dips north of the trench and lies 150 km beneath the active volcanic front. The arc is little more than 3 million years old and subduction is believed to have started 5 million years ago.

The most recent eruptions of Yali were prehistoric pumice eruptions and Methana last erupted around 230 BC. Nisyros was active until the end of the last century. Santorini on the other hand has had a considerably more active historical record and last erupted in 1950.

3.2 GEOLOGY OF SANTORINI

The oldest rocks on Santorini are Triassic slates and marbles which form a pre-volcanic basement outcropping on the southeast part of the largest island, Thera (Figure 3.2). The remaining rocks are much younger volcanics, which, apart from the Akrotiri volcanics in the south (Figure 3.2) are less than 200 000 years old. Basalt

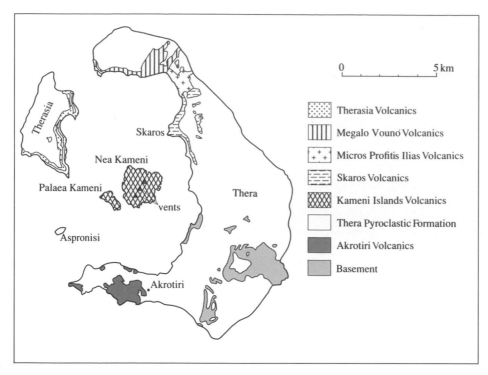

Figure 3.2 Geological map of Santorini.

Legend:
- Therasia Volcanics
- Megalo Vounó Volcanics
- Micros Profitis Ilias Volcanics
- Skaros Volcanics
- Kameni Islands Volcanics
- Thera Pyroclastic Formation
- Akrotiri Volcanics
- Basement

and andesite lava flows are common, but explosive eruptions of andesite and dacite have punctuated the volcanic history forming the Thera Pyroclastic Formation, whose most recent member blankets much of Santorini (Figure 3.2). Several of the ashfall and ignimbrite deposits have volumes of several cubic kilometres and their eruption led to caldera collapse as a result of the loss of magma from a shallow chamber. Thus, the outer shorelines of the two largest Santorini islands are on the gently sloping flanks of the volcano, while the inner shoreline is at the foot of precipitous cliffs that were generated when the centre of the volcano experienced caldera collapse (Figure 3.3).

Figure 3.3 Northward view of the eastern caldera wall and rim, Santorini. The gently sloping flank of the volcano dips to the right (east). In the foreground, the pale rocks are pumiceous airfall and pyroclastic flow deposits of the Minoan eruption (*c.* 3 500 years ago). Beneath them the caldera wall exposes older lava flows. The cliffs are about 250 m high.

The most famous eruption of Santorini occurred about 3 500 years ago. The pumice deposits which it generated covered the village of Akrotiri, an outpost of the Minoan civilization and now an important archaeological site (Figure 3.2). The demise of Minoan civilization on Crete and the destruction of the mythical city of Atlantis have been attributed to the effects of this caldera-forming eruption, which has become known as the Minoan eruption. Although scholars have failed to verify these legends, it is known that the populace of Akrotiri had left before the catastrophic phase of the Minoan eruption overwhelmed their township. No human skeletons have been uncovered by the archaeological excavations. The eruption of a thin (1 to 4 cm) but rarely exposed ash layer seems to have alerted the islanders to the possibility of further explosions and so prompted their exodus. Minor eruptions often, but not always, precede major eruptions of gas-rich magma at inter-mediate and acidic volcanoes—a useful but enigmatic signal of imminent activity to present-day volcano surveillance teams. Minoan pumice layers blanket the surface of Santorini to depths of several metres and include pyroclastic flow deposits.

After the Minoan eruption and the related caldera collapse, the volcano started to grow again by the eruption of dacite lavas. These built the two small islands of Palaea Kameni and Nea Kameni (translated as old and new smoking islands, respectively), which are shown in Figures 3.2 and 3.4. The oldest exposed lava dates from 197 BC, and the youngest from 1950. The vents of many of the Kameni lavas are localized along a NE–SW trend (Figure 3.2), roughly parallel with dykes that are now exposed in the northeast part of the caldera wall.

Figure 3.4 View of Nea Kameni from the cliffs on the eastern side of the caldera. Lavas of different ages are identifiable on the basis of different degrees of weathering and vegetation. The southern tip of Therasia, on the western side of the caldera, and Aspronisi are seen in the background.

The concentration of activity on fracture-controlled lineaments throughout much of Santorini's history seems to have led to the volcano growing as a collection of separate shield or lava cones rather than as a single towering composite volcano. Thus, in the northern part of the islands, four volcanic centres—Micros Profitis Ilias, Therasia, Megalo Vouno and Skaros—have been recognized from the present-day exposures in the caldera cliffs (Figure 3.2). A W–E cross-section in pre-Minoan times would have looked similar to Figure 3.5a, showing the overlapping lava fields and the cross-cutting nature of the feeder dykes. Today, the same area, seen in cross-section (Figure 3.5b) shows the effect of the Minoan eruption—engulfment of the central part of the volcanic complex by the sea caused by caldera formation, and the blanketing of the remnants of the volcano with layers of pumice and ash. The deposits and effects of volcanic eruptions on Santorini are explored further in VC 272, *Island Arc Magmatism: Santorini*. Before viewing this, however, we recommend that you read the rest of Section 3 in order to get a feel for the magmatic processes which are also discussed in the video.

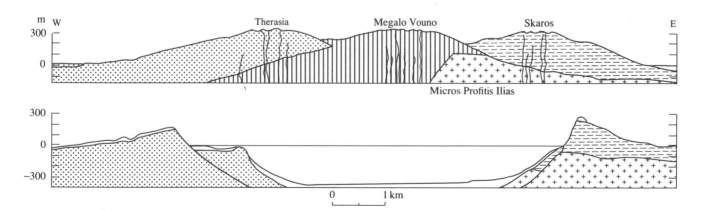

Figure 3.5 West–east cross section of northern Santorini, showing (a) the overlapping lava cones of Therasia, Megalo Vouno, Micros Profitis Ilias and Skaros prior to caldera formation, and (b) the present-day structure showing the islands of Therasia and Thera as the remnants of the older cones and now blanketed by Minoan pumice. Key as for Figure 3.2.

What goes on beneath the volcano? Since volcanic rocks are quenched samples of liquid erupted from a magma chamber, they can help us to answer this question. The clearest picture will emerge if we confine ourselves to studying a set of fresh, unweathered, samples. The lavas of the Skaros volcano are particularly well exposed in cliff sections (Figure 3.6), so that rocks from the volcano's history can be collected in correct stratigraphic order. This has advantages over collecting samples from the surface or flanks of a volcano, since we can reach deeper and therefore older rocks.

Figure 3.6 View of the Skaros lava flows, exposed in 300 m high caldera walls.

3.3 THE NATURE OF THE SKAROS VOLCANIC ROCKS

3.3.1 Chemical composition

Chemical composition and mineralogy provide means of classifying volcanic rocks. Chemical composition can be used to discriminate between magmas of different tectonic settings, and the TiO_2 versus Zr diagram introduced in Block 2, Figure 4.2, can be used to show that the Skaros, and in fact all Santorini rocks, fall reassuringly in the field of subduction-zone magmas (Figure 3.7).

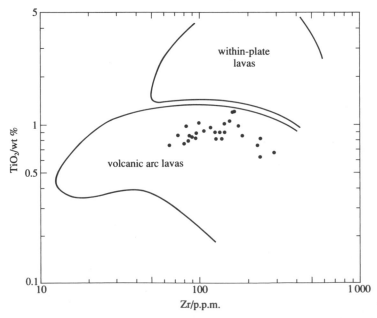

Figure 3.7 Plot of TiO_2 (wt%) against Zr (p.p.m.) showing fields of volcanic arc lavas and within-plate lavas, together with analyses of Skaros lavas (dots).

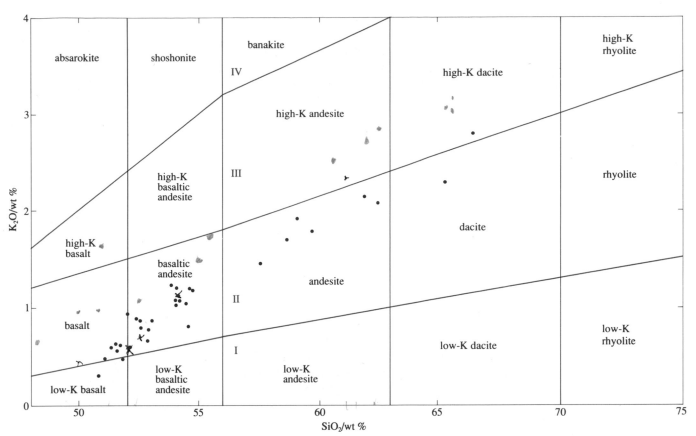

To prepare for a useful discussion of geochemistry and magmatic processes, it is necessary to first define some rock names. For subduction-related magmas, this is often done using the plot of K_2O against SiO_2, which is given in Figure 3.8, together with analyses of some Skaros lavas. The vertical lines divide the rocks into basalt, basaltic-andesite, andesite, dacite and rhyolite on the basis of their SiO_2 content. The sloping (red) lines then define the four groups I to IV. Of these groups, I to III are known as the **low-K, medium-K** and **high-K** series respectively, while group IV, an unusually potassic group of rare subduction zone magmas, are the **shoshonite series**. Magmas from a given volcanic arc generally fall in one of the low-, medium- or high-K series.

Figure 3.8 Plot of K_2O (wt%) against SiO_2 (wt%) showing the nomenclature of subduction-related magmas. The red lines divide the field into the groups labelled I to IV. Plotted points are analyses of lavas from Skaros, Santorini.

Table 3.1 Chemical composition of selected rocks from the Skaros lava pile. Major element oxides in weight percent, trace elements in parts per million (p.p.m.)

Sample Rock type	181	180	182	178	171	153
SiO_2	50.81	51.83	52.84	54.47	62.50	66.44
TiO_2	0.75	0.77	0.82	0.90	0.82	0.67
Al_2O_3	18.74	18.26	18.01	18.49	16.10	15.37
FeO_t	8.28	7.94	8.22	7.84	5.54	4.66
MnO	0.17	0.16	0.18	0.17	0.14	0.15
MgO	6.44	6.21	5.89	4.35	1.74	1.07
CaO	11.37	11.29	10.77	9.61	4.71	2.58
Na_2O	2.25	2.44	2.57	3.03	4.49	3.16
K_2O	0.31	0.48	0.66	1.04	2.07	2.79
P_2O_5	0.08	0.09	0.10	0.12	0.22	0.20
Total	99.20	99.47	100.06	100.02	98.33	99.09
Rb	9	17	22	38	69	93
Sr	221	207	212	221	188	136
Th	1.1	2.7	3.4	6.4	12.4	16.0
Ni	34	35	31	12	6	1
V	285	264	265	246	85	—
Sc	37	39	37	32	19	11

ITQ 3.1 (a) Assign the Skaros lavas to one of the groups defined in Figure 3.8.

(b) Table 3.1 lists the analyses of six representative lavas from Skaros analysed by Dr J. P. P. Huijsmans of the University of Utrecht. On the basis of their SiO_2 contents assign each rock a name, and complete the row labelled 'rock type' in Table 3.1.

The wide range in silica content of Santorini's rocks is typical of arc volcanoes, and they are said to constitute a **basalt–andesite–dacite association**.

A second widespread means of classification relies on the observation that some igneous rock series have consistently higher ratios of iron to magnesium, at a given SiO_2 content, than other igneous rock series. This difference has been capitalized on to distinguish two rock series on the basis of the ratio of the total amount of iron oxide, denoted by **FeO_t**, assuming it all to be iron(II) oxide rather than a mixture of iron(II) and iron(III) oxides, to MgO (Figure 3.9).

The total FeO content is found from the equation

$$FeO_t = 0.9Fe_2O_3 + FeO \qquad (3.1)$$

where Fe_2O_3 and FeO are given by the original analysis of the rock. The FeO_1/MgO versus SiO_2 diagram is split into two fields, as shown in Figure 3.9. Rocks with comparatively high FeO_t/MgO ratios belong to a tholeiitic series, while low FeO_t/MgO ratios imply membership of a **calc-alkaline series**. (The term calc-alkaline is inherited from an older method of classification based on the relative abundances of calcium and total alkalis, but the details of this need not concern us.)

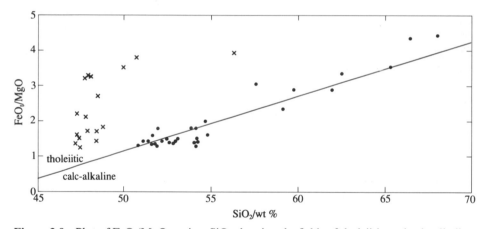

Figure 3.9 Plot of FeO_t/MgO against SiO_2 showing the fields of tholeiitic and calc-alkaline rocks. The plotted analyses are from Iceland (crosses) and Santorini (circles).

The Skaros samples straddle the dividing line in Figure 3.9, but this is not a problem. The variation diagram is still useful, because (a) it demonstrates as did Figure 3.8 that the compositions of these rocks form a clearly defined series or trend, and (b) it can show that the Skaros series has certain differences when compared with other series. For example, a series of lavas from the volcanoes of Iceland, plotted as crosses in Figure 3.9, fall on a trend that has a higher FeO_1/MgO at a given SiO_2 (within the tholeiitic field) and a different shape from that defined by the Skaros data. In your second level studies, it was found that the path followed by rocks on a variation diagram depend on (a) the amount and (b) the composition of minerals that are removed by fractional crystallization. In Figure 3.9, we could, therefore, be seeing evidence that the fractional crystallization process at Santorini, in a subduction setting, is different from that in Iceland, which sits on the mid-Atlantic constructive plate margin. The chemical composition of the rocks challenges us to understand the processes that account for their nature. This is a challenge we shall pick up shortly, but we should examine one more variation diagram before rounding off this foray into compositional nomenclature schemes.

Figure 3.10 is a ternary plot known as the **AFM diagram**, after the components

A = Na$_2$O + K$_2$O (the alkalis)

F = FeO$_t$

M = MgO

whose mutual variation it illustrates. On the AFM diagram, basalts fall close to the FM side of the triangle, far from the A apex, because these magmas are poor in alkalis compared with FeO$_t$ and MgO. Silicic magmas, being rich in alkalis and impoverished in FeO$_t$ and especially MgO, plot close to the AF side. Progressing from basalt through andesite to dacite, the Santorini and Icelandic analyses each define trends that sweep from right to left across the diagram. These trends ultimately point towards the A apex, as this is where very highly evolved silicic magmas, with low concentrations of iron and magnesium, would plot.

The AFM diagram (Figure 3.10) usefully displays a number of important points concerning tholeiitic and calc-alkaline magma compositions.

Thus intermediate members of tholeiitic magma series have high FeO$_t$/MgO ratios, as was also seen in Figure 3.9, and so plot closer to the F apex than do intermediate calc-alkaline magmas. The AFM diagram is thus divided into two regions (Figure 3.10); the upper region contains tholeiitic compositions, the lower region contains calc-alkaline compositions. The boundary between the two fields serves exactly the same purpose as the tholeiitic/calc-alkaline boundary in Figure 3.9. On both diagrams, the Icelandic rocks are defined as tholeiitic, while those of Santorini are predominantly calc-alkaline.

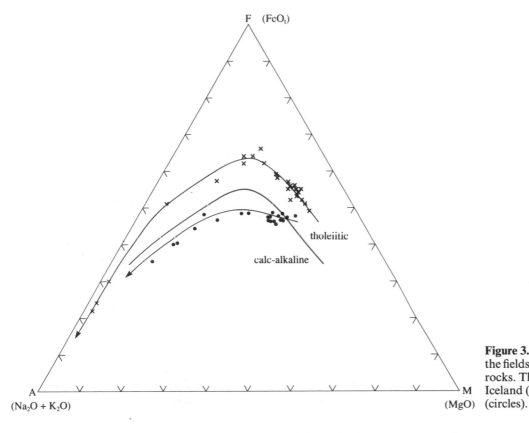

Figure 3.10 AFM diagram showing the fields of tholeiitic and calc-alkaline rocks. The plotted analyses are from Iceland (crosses) and Santorini (circles).

Tholeiitic series always display a notably arched variation trend. This is caused by a sharp rise in FeO$_t$ during the stage of differentiation from basalt to andesite—the same effect that causes FeO$_t$/MgO to rise so steeply with SiO$_2$ in Figure 3.9. Tholeiitic series, then, are characterized by a trend of iron enrichment. In contrast, calc-alkaline series define a much less humped variation trend on the AFM diagram—there is no prominent iron enrichment. This implies that calc-alkaline (subduction zone) and tholeiitic (constructive margin) magmas have different chemical evolutionary histories.

On the basis of their chemical composition, Santorini's magmas are basalts, basaltic andesites, andesites, and dacites. Together, they form a rock series that may be termed medium-K or, equivalently, calc-alkaline. For comparison, low-K series, which erupt at certain other subduction zones particularly island arcs in ocean basins, such as the Tonga and Scotia arcs (see Figure 1.1 for locations) plot in the tholeiitic fields of Figures 3.9 and 3.10.

We can also remark here on the Al_2O_3 content of subduction zone basalts (e.g. samples 181 and 180 in Table 3.1). How do these compare with basalts from other tectonic settings, such as those you studied in Block 2 (Table 5.1)? With typically more than 17% Al_2O_3, it is not surprising that subduction zone basalts often warrant the name **high-alumina basalt**.

3.3.2 Mineralogy

The Skaros lavas are typical of subduction zone volcanoes in being rather rich in crystals (25% crystals on average) and having plagioclase feldspar as the dominant phenocryst. In addition to plagioclase, all of the rocks contain the clinopyroxene augite. Basalts and some basaltic andesites contain olivine as the only other mineral, while the more silicic rocks are free from olivine but contain orthopyroxene and magnetite. This can be summarized in a diagram such as Figure 3.11, which records the presence of a given mineral in a rock of specific SiO_2 content as a filled bar. Where the bar is lightly shaded the mineral in question may or may not be present in the indicated SiO_2 range. This uncertainty cannot be avoided since there are some gaps in the SiO_2 contents of the analysed rocks. Just as chemical composition can be used to classify and name rocks, so can their mineralogy. At Santorini, the lavas usually contain either plagioclase + augite + olivine phenocrysts or plagioclase + augite + orthopyroxene + magnetite phenocrysts.

> **ITQ 3.2** (a) At what (approximate) SiO_2 content is there a change in the phenocryst assemblage in Santorini's lavas?
>
> (b) How does your answer to part (a) compare with the silica contents associated with rock name boundaries defined in Figure 3.8?

Figure 3.11 shows that the chemical composition of a lava has an influence in determining its particular mineralogy. At a more detailed level, it is found that the composition of individual minerals is also dependent on the bulk rock composition.

All of the phenocryst phases in the Skaros rocks belong to mineral groups that are solid solution series. When you studied the phase diagrams of simple binary systems showing solid solution (e.g. Fo–Fa and An–Ab) at second level, it was found that a Fo-rich liquid would precipitate an olivine that was more Fo-rich than olivine precipitated from a less Fo-rich liquid. Magmas show the same feature—an MgO-rich magma will precipitate phenocrysts of MgO-rich olivine and pyroxene. Similarly, a CaO-rich magma will precipitate anorthite-rich plagioclase phenocrysts. If the magma and its minerals are in chemical equilibrium, then there should be a close correlation between mineral and rock compositions.

The precise composition of a mineral can be found by separating it from a crushed rock sample and making a chemical analysis. However, other minerals may be accidentally included in the analysed material, being either present as inclusions within the crystals of interest or as loose crystals that failed to be separated out during sample preparation. To overcome these difficulties, a different method is required. This relies on an instrument known as the **electron microprobe**. In this technique, a thin section of rock with a highly polished surface is specially prepared and placed in a vacuum chamber. A focused beam of electrons is then directed onto an area a few micrometres across on the sample's surface. The electron beam causes this tiny region to emit X-rays of a character dependent on the chemical composition of the bombarded material. These X-rays are monitored by a detector enabling the composition of the targeted spot to be obtained. Several analyses can be made across a single crystal, building a detailed picture of any compositional zoning. This would be impossible to detect, let alone measure, by just analysing a composite sample of grains separated from the rock; such a method would only give the average

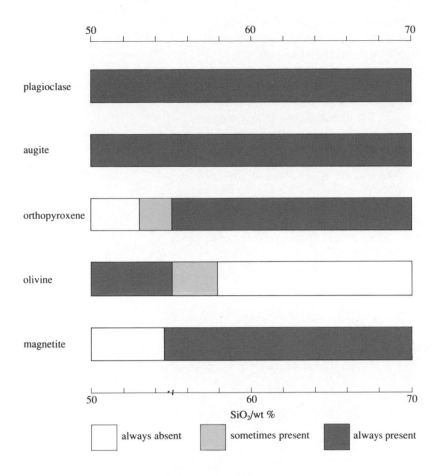

Figure 3.11 Diagrammatic summary of the correlation between modal mineralogy and rock compositions in lavas from Skaros.

composition. Using the microprobe, different crystals of the same mineral within a single thin section can be analysed to check for homogeneity. This type of detail is invaluable in unravelling many petrological problems, including certain aspects of Santorini's magmatism.

To begin with, we shall examine the composition of olivine, augite, orthopyroxene and plagioclase and relate these to the compositions of their host rocks. Most phenocrysts in the Skaros lavas are compositionally zoned—a feature that can be detected using the petrological microscope as subtle concentric changes in the interference colours of olivine and augite and concentric 'growth ring' patterns in plagioclase phenocrysts (Plate 3.1 in the CPB). However, if the cores of the phenocrysts precipitated from a liquid that is now represented by the bulk rock, then their compositions should correlate with the bulk rock's composition.

Olivine compositions are reported in terms of the proportions of forsterite (Fo: Mg_2SiO_4) and fayalite (Fa: Fe_2SiO_4). The forsterite content of olivine cores decreases with decreasing MgO in the whole rock (Figure 3.12). This correlation can be extrapolated to still more magnesian basalts, which have been found elsewhere on Santorini, and extrapolated to less magnesian rocks at the limit of the olivine crystallization range.

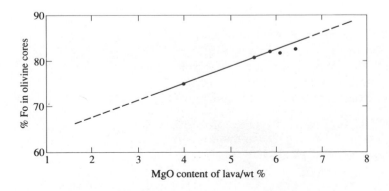

Figure 3.12 Correlation between the forsterite (Fo) content of olivine and the MgO content of their host lava. Data points are from Skaros, and the broken lines extrapolate the trend to compositions found elsewhere.

Pyroxene contains the Ca, Mg and Fe end-members wollastonite (Wo: $Ca_2Si_2O_6$), enstatite (En: $Mg_2Si_2O_6$) and ferrosilite (Fs: $Fe_2Si_2O_6$). The compositions of augite and orthopyroxene plot within the **pyroxene quadrilateral** shown in Figure 3.13 (cf. Block 2, Figure 3.2). The corners of the quadrilateral are defined by the compositions En, Fs, diopside (Di: $CaMgSi_2O_6$ i.e. $En_{50}Fs_0Wo_{50}$) and hedenbergite (Hd: $CaFeSi_2O_6$ i.e. $En_0Fs_{50}Wo_{50}$). Augite contains substantial quantities of calcium and so plots in the upper part of the quadrilateral, in the direction of the Wo corner. Orthopyroxene contains only minor amounts of calcium and so plots close to the enstatite (En)–ferrosilite (Fs) join.

Basalt contains the most magnesian augites found at Skaros, and these augites plot near the diopside (Di) corner of the pyroxene quadrilateral (Figure 3.13). Andesites and dacites contain less MgO than basalt (e.g. Table 3.1), so that pyroxenes that crystallize from these magmas plot further to the right of the pyroxene quadrilateral. Both augite and orthopyroxene are present in these more evolved magmas, and in Figure 3.13, tie lines join the co-existing pyroxene compositions to illustrate the shift to less magnesian mineral compositions with degreasing MgO in the rock.

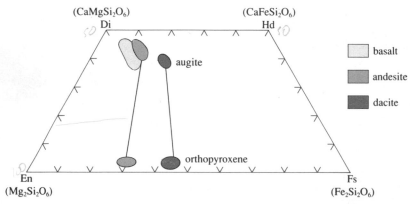

Figure 3.13 The pyroxene quadrilateral, showing the compositions of augite in basalt, andesite and dacite, and of orthopyroxene in andesite and dacite. Tie lines join coexisting augite and orthopyroxene compositions.

To relate a pyroxene crystal's composition to its position to the left (Mg-rich) or right (Fe-rich) of Figure 3.13, it is convenient to quote its **Mg ratio**. This is a number which is defined as:

$$\text{Mg ratio} = 100 \times \text{Mg}/(\text{Mg} + \text{Fe}) \tag{3.2}$$

or, equivalently,

$$\text{Mg ratio} = 100 \times \text{En}/(\text{En} + \text{Fs}) \tag{3.3}$$

since En and Fs are the pure Mg and Fe end members.

> **ITQ 3.3** (a) One of the basalts from Skaros contains augite of composition $En_{47.1}Fs_{12.4}Wo_{40.5}$. What is the Mg ratio of this crystal?
>
> (b) Estimate, using Figure 3.13, the composition of augite in Skaros dacite and determine its Mg ratio.

Will the Mg ratio of pyroxenes increase or decrease with MgO content of the host rock? Augite compositions from a number of Skaros lavas are shown plotted against their host rocks' MgO content in Figure 3.14. The correlation that emerges from Figure 3.14 is similar to that found with the olivines. A magma with a low MgO content will precipitate ferromagnesian minerals that are poor in magnesium.

Plagioclase composition also depends on the composition of the bulk rock. This relationship is summarized in Table 3.2. So, in parallel with a decrease in the Mg ratio of ferromagnesian minerals, the anorthite content of plagioclase phenocrysts decreases in more evolved magmas.

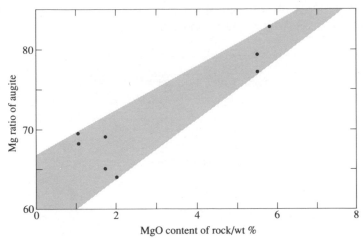

Figure 3.14 Plot showing the correlation between the Mg ratio of augite in Skaros lavas and the MgO content of the host rock.

Table 3.2 Correlation between the composition of plagioclase and its host rock among Skaros lavas

Rock type	Wt % SiO$_2$ in rock	Wt % CaO in rock	Anorthite content of plagioclase
basalt	< 52	> 10.5	94–75
basaltic andesite	52–56	8–10.5	89–71
andesite	56–63	4–8	80–50
dacite	> 63	< 4	65–40

These observations can be summarized as reflecting chemical equilibrium between each mineral and the melt from which it grew. Later, we shall discover examples where this does not hold. However, the present set of 'equilibrium' rocks are examined further in the next Section.

3.4 FRACTIONAL CRYSTALLIZATION

We have already found that the compositional variation among the Skaros lavas is not random but shows good correlations between certain elements (Figures 3.8 to 3.10). We would, therefore, expect that a systematic process, rather than a random process, must be responsible for determining all of the magmas' compositions. Fractional crystallization is one such process, and operates as follows. As a magma cools and crystallizes, elements that are preferentially incorporated into the growing crystals become impoverished in the remaining melt. Similarly, elements that are not incorporated into the crystals become enriched in the remaining liquid. By separating the crystals from the liquid, a new magma with a different composition will be produced. This is fractional crystallization. By this process, basaltic magma can give rise to basaltic andesites, which can in turn produce andesite and still more acidic, fractionated (or evolved) magmas. These principles were introduced during second level courses, along with mixing calculations to interpret variation diagrams in terms of the generation of a new magma by the subtraction of phenocrysts from a primitive magma.

Figure 3.15 is a variation diagram showing the compositions of Skaros lavas and minerals. Can you determine whether it is feasible to derive andesite with 57% SiO$_2$ by the removal of plagioclase, augite and olivine from basalt with 51% SiO$_2$?

24

ITQ 3.4 (a) What is the approximate Al_2O_3 content of the plagioclase +
augite + olivine mineral extract that would be required to generate the andesite
from the basalt?

(b) Estimate the proportion of plagioclase in the mineral extract.

(c) How might the kink in the Al_2O_3 versus SiO_2 trend at $SiO_2 \approx 57\%$ have
originated?

In answering ITQ 3.4, you will have found that the major element variation diagram
(Figure 3.15) is suggestive of fractional crystallization at Skaros. However, definite
conclusions are difficult to come to because the compositions of the minerals that are
assumed to be fractionating from the magma do not have unique compositions. This
reflects the fact, which we discovered from Figures 3.12 to 3.14, that the composition
of a mineral depends on the composition of the magma from which it crystallizes.

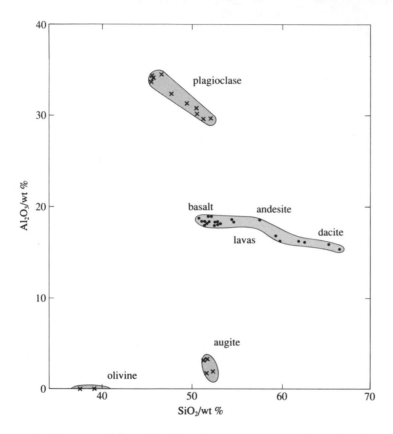

Figure 3.15 Variation diagram
of Al_2O_3 against SiO_2. Points are
analysed lavas from Skaros, and
crosses are minerals in basalt lava.

Consequently, the composition of a mineral extract must continuously change as the
composition of the residual liquid is changing. This complicates the calculation of
fractional crystallization effects using major elements. Could there be an alternative
to using major elements?

It turns out that trace elements provide a much more useful tool with which to
investigate magmatic processes. The remainder of this Section is devoted to the use
of trace elements in the study of fractional crystallization. Our approach is to predict how the abundances of various trace elements will change during fractional
crystallization and then to test our predictions with real data from Skaros.

3.4.1 The Rayleigh fractionation equation

Trace elements are used widely in studies of igneous processes, and you were introduced to some of their uses in second level courses and in Block 2. In those previous
studies, you found that the concentration of a given trace element in an igneous
mineral was proportional to that trace element's concentration in the liquid from
which the mineral was growing. The constant of proportionality is known as the
partition coefficient, K_D, defined as

$$K_D = \frac{\text{concentration of trace element in mineral}}{\text{concentration of trace element in liquid}} \quad (3.4)$$

Also, the concentration of a trace element in an assemblage of different minerals is similarly related to the concentration in the liquid, but here we refer to the bulk partition coefficient, D, where

$$D = \frac{\text{concentration of trace element in mineral assemblage}}{\text{concentration of trace element in liquid}} \qquad (3.5)$$

For an assemblage of three minerals α, β and γ that are present in mass fractions (i.e. proportions by mass) X_α, X_β and X_γ and have partition coefficients $K_{D,\alpha}$, $K_{D,\beta}$, and $K_{D,\gamma}$, we have

$$D = X_\alpha K_{D,\alpha} + X_\beta K_{D,\beta} + X_\gamma K_{D,\gamma} \qquad (3.6)$$

ITQ 3.5 Consider the trace element nickel (Ni) and a mineral assemblage consisting of 60% plagioclase, 10% augite and 30% olivine. The partition coefficients for Ni between these minerals and liquid are 0.01, 2.0 and 6.2 respectively. (a) Calculate the bulk partition coefficient of Ni, D_{Ni}, for this mineral assemblage.

(b) According to your answer to part (a) will there be a greater or lesser concentration of Ni in the mineral assemblage than in the co-existing liquid?

A trace element that preferentially enters the solid phase (i.e. $K_D > 1$ or $D > 1$) is said to be a compatible trace element. On the other hand, an incompatible trace element is one that preferentially remains in the liquid phase (i.e. $K_D < 1$ or $D < 1$).

During fractional crystallization, early-formed crystals (and the trace elements they contain) are continuously removed from chemical contact with the residual liquid. The amount of a trace element in the liquid therefore changes in concentration from the original amount, C_0, to some new amount C_1. C_1 depends on C_0, D, and also on how much liquid is still left, F. The equation that relates these variables was derived by Lord Rayleigh in 1896, and is

$$C_1 = C_0 F^{(D-1)} \qquad (3.7a)$$

You will recall meeting equation 3.7 in Block 2 (equation 4.2); it is known as the **Rayleigh fractionation equation**, and is one of the most widely used equations in igneous petrology. We will use this equation to see how trace element concentrations are expected to change as a result of fractional crystallization. It will then be possible for us to examine analyses from a suite of volcanic rocks (which are assumed to be quenched magmatic liquids) and determine whether or not fractional crystallization has been operating at that volcano.

First of all, consider how the enrichment or depletion of a trace element varies with the amount of crystallization. Values of C_1/C_0 are calculated from the equation

$$\frac{C_1}{C_0} = F^{(D-1)} \qquad (3.7b)$$

which is just equation 3.7 after dividing both sides by C_0. So, we have

for $D=3$, $\quad C_1/C_0 = F^2$
for $D=2$, $\quad C_1/C_0 = F^1 = F$
for $D=1$, $\quad C_1/C_0 = F^0 = 1$
for $D=0$, $\quad C_1/C_0 = F^{-1} = 1/F$

Table 3.3 lists C_1/C_0 as a function of F and D, for $D=3, 2, 1$ and 0. We have left you to work out the values that should go in the blank spaces in this Table.

ITQ 3.6 Complete the listing of C_1/C_0 values in Table 3.3.

It is easier to discuss these results after plotting them on a graph.

ITQ 3.7   Plot the data points from your completed Table 3.3 onto Figure 3.16 so as to derive curves of C_l/C_o as a function for F for each value of the bulk partition coefficient, D. (Hint: work systematically by plotting all of the data for one D value, then draw a smooth curve through the set of data points before plotting the values for the next D value.)

The interpretation of your completed Figure 3.16 diagram is very simple. Compatible elements are depleted ($C_l/C_o < 1$) and become depleted most rapidly the larger D is. Incompatible elements increase in concentration with differentiation. However, D can never have a value less than 0, so in this model of fractional crystallization, the concentration of any trace element can never plot above the curve labelled $D = 0$.

The easiest way to learn the Rayleigh fractionation equation is to use it, for example by answering the following ITQ.

ITQ 3.8   (a) Consider a parental basalt containing 5 parts per million (p.p.m.) Rb. Fractional cystallization of olivine, plagioclase and clinopyroxene produces andesite magma with 16 p.p.m. Rb. If the bulk partition coefficient for Rb is $D_{Rb} = 0$, what proportion of the original basalt does the fractionated magma represent (i.e. what is F)?

(b) The same basalt contains 100 p.p.m. Ni and has $D_{Ni} = 2.0$; the andesite has 31 p.p.m. Ni. Does this fit in with your result from (a)?

Table 3.3   Normalized liquid composition C_l/C_o as a function of the fraction of liquid remaining F, during Rayleigh fractionation with bulk partition coefficient D

F	$D = 3$	$D = 2$	$D = 1$	$D = 0$
1	1.00	1.00	1.00	1.00
0.9	0.81	0.90	1.00	1.11
0.8	0.64	0.80	1.00	1.25
0.7	0.49	0.7	1.00	1.43
0.6	0.36	0.60	1.00	1.67
0.5	0.25	0.50	1.00	2.00
0.4	0.16	0.40	1.00	2.50
0.3	0.09	0.30	1.00	3.33
0.2	0.04	0.20	1.00	5.00
0.1	0.01	0.10	1.00	10.00

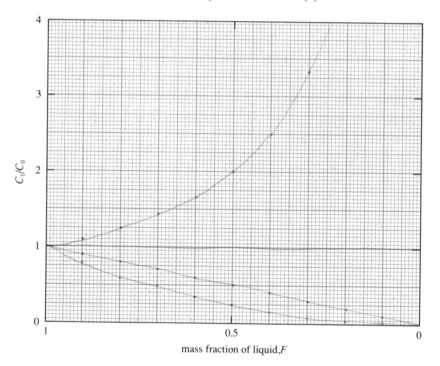

Figure 3.16   Graphical representation of the Rayleigh fractionation law (for use with ITQ 3.7).

mass fraction of liquid, F

You should be convinced that the Rayleigh fractionation equation can explain the composition of the andesite in ITQ 3.8. To test all of the members of an entire rock series for evidence of fractional crystallization using the method of ITQ 3.8 would be very tedious, especially if we had to consider many trace elements. We need a streamlined way of testing for fractional crystallization in a rock series. Instead of considering one element at a time, we can take a shortcut and simultaneously treat two elements.

Note, from Table 3.3 or Figure 3.16, that for every F value, the values of C_l/C_o depends on the value of D. If we take two elements, say Rb and Ni which you examined in ITQ 3.8, whose D values are known, then we can plot a graph of Rb/Rb_o against Ni/Ni_o using the data given in Table 3.3.

ITQ 3.9   Complete a graph of Ni/Ni_o (assuming $D_{Ni} = 2.0$) against Rb/Rb_o (assuming $D_{Rb} = 0$) by plotting the relevant C_l/C_o values contained in Table 3.3 onto Figure 3.17, and draw a curve through the data.

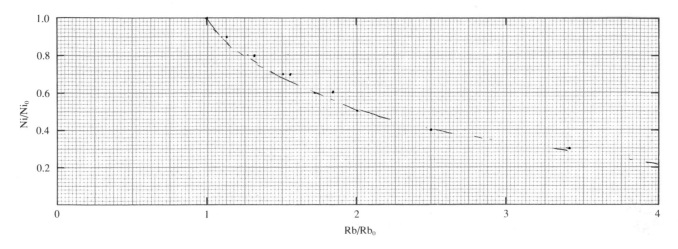

Figure 3.17 Graph of Ni/Ni_o (assuming $D_{Ni} = 2.0$) against Rb/Rb_o (assuming $D_{Rb} = 0$). For use with ITQ 3.9.

Make sure that you have plotted the correct curve by checking your answer now. Note that the behaviours of the two elements are completely different. Rb increases in abundance, while Ni decreases with Rayleigh fractionation leading to a specific concave curve on the variation diagram.

> **ITQ 3.10**   Recall the parental basalt with Ni ($= Ni_o$) $= 100$ p.p.m. and Rb ($= Rb_o$) $= 5$ p.p.m. that we considered in ITQ 3.8. Which of the following compositions cannot be derived by fractional crystallization from that parental basalt (assuming $D_{Ni} = 2.0$ and $D_{Rb} = 0.0$)?
> A   Ni $= 71$, Rb $= 7$
> B   Ni $= 50$, Rb $= 10$
> C   Ni $- 45$, Rb $= 13$
> D   Ni $= 89$, Rb $= 7$

You should also be able to see that the Ni/Ni_o and Rb/Rb_o ratios of the andesite of ITQ 3.8 plot on the curve you drew onto Figure 3.17, confirming the role of fractional crystallization. The data in ITQs 3.8 and 3.10 either fall on the fractionation curve of Figure 3.17 (in which case they represent magmas generated by fractional crystallization from a parent with $Ni_o = 100$ p.p.m., $Rb_o = 5$ p.p.m.) or off the fractionation curve (implying that they owe their origin to some other process or parental magma). We are finding that rather than making repetitive calculations, there are graphical ways of testing for fractional crystallization. These graphical methods rely simply on plotting trace element analyses and comparing their positions with the values that fractional crystallization (the Rayleigh fractionation equation) predicts. Thus, analyses of a suite of lavas will plot along a curve such as that in Figure 3.17 only if they are related by fractional crystallization from the same parent. Failure to plot on such a curve indicates that some other process or processes must have operated in the magma chamber.

> Your completed Figure 3.17 (Figure A2) is a 'standard fractionation curve' with which to compare real analytical data, but can you see any practical problems with using this diagram?

Figure A2 gives a specific picture of Rayleigh fractionation—it applies to the case where two elements have $D = 2$ and $D = 0$, and we would also need to know Ni_o and Rb_o (or in general the C_o values) before we could plot any data. To be more useful, we need a more general diagram to describe the Rayleigh fractionation law. Such a diagram requires the use of logarithms. For completeness, the algebra that shows why this is necessary is given below, but you do not need to be able to follow the mathematics. What you will need to understand is the conclusion, which is set out in words after the algebra.

28

Taking the logarithms of the Rayleigh equation (equation 3.7), we get

$$\log C_1 = \log C_o + (D-1) \log F \qquad (3.8)$$

so for Rb:

$$\log Rb = \log Rb_o + (D_{Rb}-1) \log F \qquad (3.9)$$

and for Ni:

$$\log Ni = \log Ni_o + (D_{Ni}-1) \log F \qquad (3.10)$$

The term $\log F$ is easily eliminated from equations 3.9 and 3.10 to give us

$$\log Ni = \left(\frac{D_{Ni}-1}{D_{Rb}-1}\right) \log Rb + \log Ni_o - \left(\frac{D_{Ni}-1}{D_{Rb}-1}\right) \log Rb_o \qquad (3.11)$$

This may look a totally unmanageable equation, but all we need to see is that it is the equation of a straight line

$$y = mx + c$$
$$\text{where } y = \log Ni$$
$$m = \left(\frac{D_{Ni}-1}{D_{Rb}-1}\right) \qquad (3.12)$$
$$x = \log Rb$$

$$c = \log Ni_o - \left(\frac{D_{Ni}-1}{D_{Rb}-1}\right) \log Rb_o \qquad (3.13)$$

These complicated-looking equations state the simple conclusion that *magmas related by fractional crystallization will have trace element abundances that lie on a straight line when they are plotted on logarithmic graph paper*. This is the key test for fractional crystallization. To illustrate the usefulness of this approach, Figures 3.18a and 3.18b show the fractionation trend between Ni and Rb for the example we have been considering in ITQs 3.8 to 3.10.

For reference, Figure 3.18a shows Ni plotted against Rb on linear graph paper, revealing a curved trend, similar in shape to that of Figure 3.17. Figure 3.18b shows the same compositional trend, but plotted on logarithmic graph paper. (This has

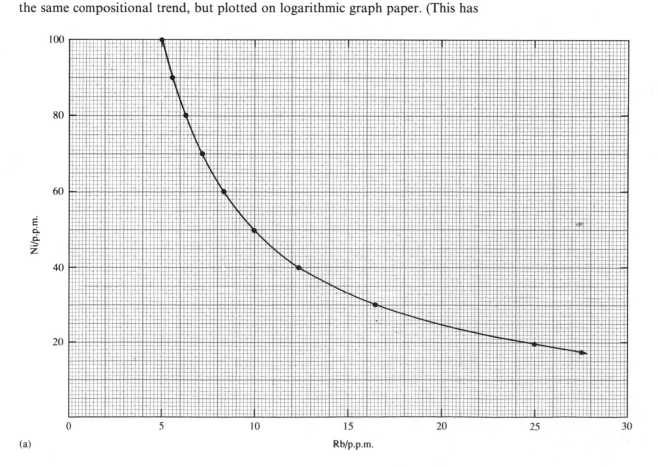

(a)

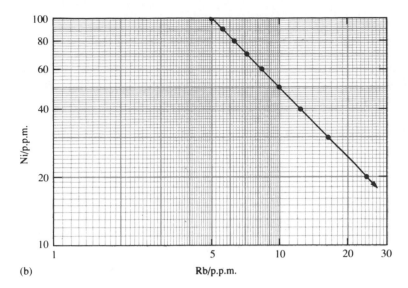

(b)

Rb/p.p.m.

Figure 3.18 Fractionation trend of magma derived from a parent basalt with $Ni_o = 100$ p.p.m., $Rb_o = 5$ p.p.m. by fractional crystallization, when $D_{Ni} = 2$ and $D_{Rb} = 0$. (a) Plotted on linear graph paper, (b) plotted on logarithmic graph paper.

the effect of squeezing together the data points at high concentrations and stretching out points at low concentrations.) The result is that the curvature of Figure 3.18a is removed, leaving a straight line—the easily identified hallmark of fractional crystallization.

In practice, we need to plot as wide a range of concentrations as possible, otherwise we would end up with a very short spread of points and it would be difficult to decide whether we were looking at a straight line or just a short segment of a curve. So, *when testing a set of geochemical data for evidence of fractional crystallization, it is best to plot the most compatible element (largest D) against the most incompatible (smallest D)*. This will ensure that the maximum variation in composition is being taken into account.

An extra result that comes out of the plot on logarithmic graph paper is that the slope of the straight-line fractionation trend is directly related to the bulk partition coefficients of the two plotted elements (equation 3.12).

> **ITQ 3.11** Using a ruler, measure the slope of the straight line in Figure 3.18b.

The anticipated slope is, from equation 3.12,

$$m = \frac{D_{Ni} - 1}{D_{Rb} - 1} = \frac{2 - 1}{0 - 1} = -1$$

and this should tally with your answer to ITQ 3.11. If you obtained a different answer, it is important that you check your calculation of the gradient by referring to the answer to ITQ 3.11.

Summary

Correlations between the abundances of trace elements in a suite of magmas will conform to a specific pattern if fractional crystallization has been operative. This pattern is defined by the Rayleigh fractionation equation (equation 3.7) relating the change in abundance of a given trace element to that element's bulk partition coefficient, D, and the mass fraction of liquid remaining after crystallization, F. Rayleigh fractionation is the only process which can produce a straight-line trend on a log–log plot of an incompatible trace element against a compatible trace element (Figure 3.18b). These trends can be interpreted in terms of bulk partition coefficients (equation 3.12). If data do not plot on a straight line, we must suspect some other process to have influenced the rocks' compositions.

3.4.2 Applying the Rayleigh fractionation equation to the trace element compositions of Skaros lavas

In this Section, we want to apply the techniques developed in the previous Section to investigate the magmatic processes associated with the Skaros lavas. The compositions of a representative set of these rocks were listed in Table 3.1. Concentrating on the trace elements, you will notice that some increase (Rb, Th) while others (Ni, V, Sc) decrease as the silica content increases. Sr remains rather constant over the range basalt to andesite, but becomes relatively impoverished in the most silicic rocks.

To test for evidence of fractional crystallization, we must plot a log–log variation diagram of a compatible trace element against an incompatible trace element. Since we are looking for the maximum compositional variation, the two elements we should plot are those showing the greatest depletion and the greatest enrichment. In this example, it is obviously Ni that shows the greatest depletion. In fact, the dacite contains 1/34 as much Ni as the basalt.

> Which trace element shows the greatest enrichment over the range basalt to dacite, using the data in Table 3.1?

You should have selected thorium as the element to plot against Ni. Data from Skaros, including those in Table 3.1, are plotted on Figure 3.19.

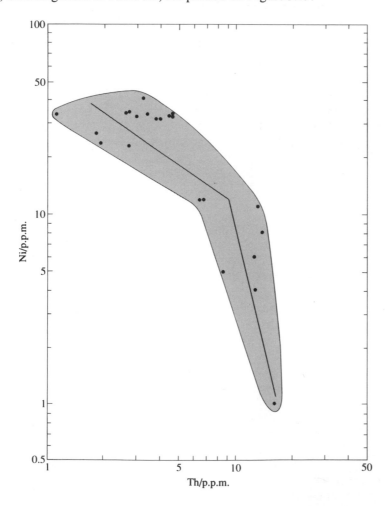

Figure 3.19 Log–log plot of Ni versus Th in Skaros lavas.

To help in appreciating the pattern shown by the data, a shaded 'balloon' has been drawn to enclose the data points. A continuous straight line cannot be drawn through the data.

Although Ni decreases as Th increases, the slope of this trend depends on whether we are dealing with basic (low Th) or acidic (high Th) rocks. Likewise, the abundances of all the other compatible trace elements (V, Sc, Sr) decrease gradually with increasing Th in the mafic rocks and more sharply in the silicic rocks (Figure 3.20).

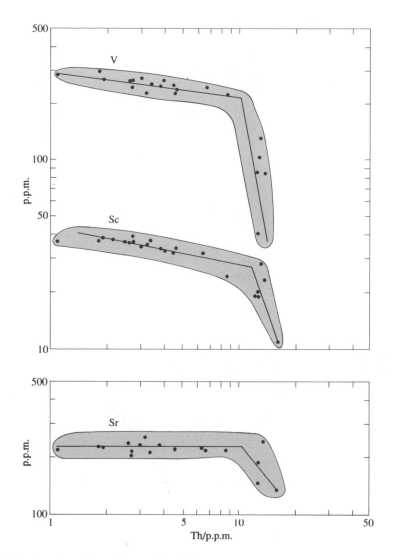

Figure 3.20 Log–log plots of vanadium (V), scandium (Sc) and strontium (Sr) against thorium (Th).

So, does the absence of a straight line through all the data mean that fractional crystallization was an insignificant process in the genesis of these Skaros lavas?

Look more closely at Figures 3.19 and 3.20. Do the data points cluster around a smoothly curved trend or is there a definite break in slope?

The variation diagrams look as if they consist of two intersecting straight lines. Since a straight line on a log–log trace element plot indicates fractional crystallization, the data from Skaros might be interpreted in terms of two stages of fractional crystallization. This idea can be illustrated with reference to Figure 3.21, which shows the compositions of three magmas labelled A, B, and C within a magma series. Starting with magma A, fractional crystallization will produce residual magmas whose compositions fall on the straight line AB. The slope of AB depends on the bulk partition coefficients of the plotted trace elements (Figure 3.18b and equation 3.13). Once the magma has evolved to a composition B, the partition coefficients change, and more fractional crystallization then gives compositions on a straight line with a different slope, in this case the line BC.

ITQ 3.12 Explain why it is possible for different magma compositions to have different bulk partition coefficients.

Returning to the patterns shown by Skaros rocks (Figures 3.19 and 3.20), can we justify the suggestion that two stages of fractional crystallization may have taken place?

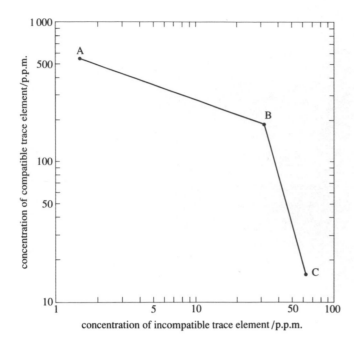

Figure 3.21 Schematic log–log trace element variation diagram illustrating the fractionation path of parental magma A in which the bulk partition coefficients in compositions more evolved than magma B are different from those in less evolved magmas.

Recall that the lavas with less than about 55% SiO_2 contain phenocrysts of plagioclase, augite, and olivine. Lavas with more than about 58% SiO_2 contain phenocrysts of plagioclase, augite, orthopyroxene and magnetite (Figure 3.11).

> **ITQ 3.13** (a) Using the analyses given in Table 3.1, estimate the Th content of Skaros lavas with 55 to 58% SiO_2.
>
> (b) How does your answer to (a) compare with the Th content at which the bulk partition coefficients in the Skaros lava series are inferred to change?

The inflections in the variation diagrams (Figures 3.19 and 3.20) thus coincide with the disappearance of olivine and the appearance of orthopyroxene and magnetite in the phenocryst assemblage of Skaros lavas. The mineralogy of the rocks thus suggests that fractional crystallization of basalt involving the removal of plagioclase, augite, and olivine may produce basaltic-andesites and andesites, while further fractional crystallization of andesite involving the removal of plagioclase, augite, orthopyroxene and magnetite can produce dacites. The basalt to andesite, and andesite to dacite compositional trends have different slopes because the fractionating assemblages, and therefore bulk partition coefficients, are different.

3.4.3 Proportions of minerals in a fractionating assemblage

Having just made a good case that fractional crystallization was an important process in the Skaros magmas, it is possible to use the Rayleigh fractionation equation to discover the proportions of the different minerals in the fractionating assemblage. This can be seen by first recalling that D is a function of the proportions

Table 3.4 Partition coefficients between plagioclase, augite, and olivine and mafic liquid

	Plagioclase	Augite	Olivine
K_{Th}	0.01	0.01	0.01
K_{Ni}	0.01	2.0	6.2
K_{Sc}	0.03	4.2	0.3
K_{Sr}	1.9	0.1	0.01
K_{V}	0.10	3.8	0.05

(X) and partition coefficients (K_D) of the fractionating minerals (equation 3.6). Now, values of K_D are available in the scientific literature, while values for D can be found by measuring the slopes of trace element trends on variation diagrams such as Figures 3.18b, 3.19 and 3.20. This leaves the mineral proportions (X values) as unknowns, so that it is theoretically possible to work back to find values of X given D and the appropriate values of K_D. One method for doing this can be illustrated by considering the Skaros magmas between basalt and basaltic-andesite, and which involve only plagioclase, augite and olivine. Partition coefficients between these minerals and basic magma are listed in Table 3.4.

These are used to define the bulk partition coefficient for each element, as given by equation (3.6). For Th (thorium):

$$
\begin{aligned}
D_{Th} &= X_{plagioclase} K_{Th}^{plagioclase/liquid} + X_{augite} K_{Th}^{augite/liquid} + X_{olivine} K_{Th}^{olivine/liquid} \\
&= X_{plagioclase} \times 0.01 + X_{augite} \times 0.01 + X_{olivine} \times 0.01 \\
&= (X_{plagioclase} + X_{augite} + X_{olivine}) \times 0.01 \\
&= 1 \times 0.01 \\
&= 0.01
\end{aligned}
$$

Thorium is thus a highly incompatible element, which is exactly what we found when examining Table 3.1 at the beginning of the previous Section. In fact, D_{Th} is so small, it is simplest to take $D_{Th} = 0$. By the same token it follows that minerals with very low partition coefficients will contribute little to the bulk partition coefficient of the fractionating assemblage. For example, Table 3.4 reveals that $K_{Ni}^{plagioclase/liquid}$ is tiny in comparison to $K_{Ni}^{olivine/liquid}$ or $K_{Ni}^{augite/liquid}$, so we can make the simple approximation

$$
D_{Ni} = X_{augite} K_{Ni}^{augite/liquid} + X_{olivine} K_{Ni}^{olivine/liquid}
$$

and similarly

$$
\begin{aligned}
D_{Sc} &= X_{augite} K_{Sc}^{augite/liquid} \\
D_{Sr} &= X_{plagioclase} K_{Sr}^{plagioclase/liquid} \\
D_{V} &= X_{augite} K_{V}^{augite/liquid}
\end{aligned}
$$

For the particular partition coefficients given in Table 3.4, we have

$$D_{Ni} = 2X_{augite} + 6.2X_{olivine} \tag{3.14}$$

$$D_{Sc} = 4.2X_{augite} \tag{3.15}$$

$$D_{Sr} = 1.9X_{plagioclase} \tag{3.16}$$

$$D_{V} = 3.8X_{augite} \tag{3.17}$$

These are much simpler equations than the more general equation 3.6, making it easier for us to work out what the mass fractions of plagioclase, augite and olivine are in the Skaros fractionation assemblage. This simplification relies on the fact that certain trace elements partition strongly into only one or two minerals in a given assemblage. The large K_D values for these minerals determine how large the bulk distribution coefficients, D, will be. Consequently, the overall behaviour of Ni during fractional crystallization is governed mainly by the amount of olivine (and to an extent augite) being removed, Sr is governed by plagioclase, and Sc and V by augite.

The behaviour of Ni in the Skaros basalts and basaltic andesites is defined by the slope of the log Ni versus log Th plot (Figure 3.19) where Th $\leqslant 10$ p.p.m. The slope of this straight line is -0.69, so from equation 3.12

$$-0.69 = \frac{D_{Ni} - 1}{D_{Th} - 1}$$

Importantly, we already know that $D_{Th} = 0$, so we can find a unique value for D_{Ni} in these magmas:

$$-0.69 = \frac{D_{Ni} - 1}{-1}$$

$$D_{Ni} = 1.69$$

Thus *the bulk partition coefficient of a given trace element can be found from the slope of a log–log diagram in which the trace element is plotted against a highly incompatible trace element (i.e. one with D=0).*

ITQ 3.14 Determine the bulk partition coefficients of V, Sc and Sr in Skaros basalts and basaltic andesites by using the straight line trends of Figure 3.20.

Your answers to ITQ 3.14 can now be put into equations 3.15 to 3.17, and, with the result for Ni, give us

$$1.69 = 2X_{\text{augite}} + 6.2X_{\text{olivine}} \tag{3.18}$$

$$1.19 = 4.2X_{\text{augite}} \tag{3.19}$$

$$1.0 \ = 1.9X_{\text{plagioclase}} \tag{3.20}$$

$$1.14 = 3.8X_{\text{augite}} \tag{3.21}$$

You can now complete the calculation of mineral proportions by working out the values of X in equations 3.18 to 3.21.

ITQ 3.15 What are the calculated proportions of plagioclase, augite and olivine in the fractionating assemblage of the Skaros basalts?

The total amount of minerals, $X_{\text{plagioclase}} + X_{\text{augite}} + X_{\text{olivine}}$, add up to 1.0, which is just as it should be if we have correctly accounted for all the minerals present.

In summary, the trace element compositions of the basaltic and basaltic-andesite members of the Skaros rock series can be explained by Rayleigh fractionation (since log–log variation diagrams define reasonable straight-line trends). Furthermore, the bulk partition coefficients implied by the analytical data have been combined with known partition coefficients for the observed phenocryst phases to calculate the proportions (by weight) of the fractionating assemblage that produces basaltic andesite from basalt. This assemblage comprises 53% plagioclase, 29% augite and 18% olivine.

Can you think of any other lines of evidence (apart from trace elements) that might support this result?

The major element compositions of lavas and minerals plotted in Figure 3.15 suggested (ITQ 3.4) that plagioclase might account for 50 to 60% of a fractionating assemblage. This supports our conclusions from the trace elements.

However, remember that the conclusions from the major element plot were rather vague because the mineral analyses showed quite a range, due to solid solution and compositional zoning, making it difficult to pick truly representative mineral compositions with which to model fractional crystallization. This problem is overcome by the trace element approach in which mineral and liquid compositions are closely linked through well-defined K_D values. Consequently, the straight line trends on log–log trace element variation diagrams that stem from the operation of Rayleigh fractionation are often easier to interpret than major element plots.

The fractionation trend between the andesites and dacites of Skaros can be treated in the same sort of ways as you have done with the basalt to basaltic andesite trend. In this case, the fractionating assemblage is found to comprise 68% plagioclase, 14% augite, 5% orthopyroxene and 11% magnetite. Thus, plagioclase makes up a large proportion of the fractionating mineral assemblage in all Skaros magmas. This fits quite nicely with the observation that all of the lavas have plagioclase as the dominant phenocryst phase.

A particular value of the trace element abundances in igneous rock series is in testing for the operation of Rayleigh fractionation within a sub-volcanic magma chamber (Section 3.4.1). Trace element modelling shows that among the Skaros lavas, basaltic andesites are derived from basalt by fractional crystallization, and that the basaltic andesites undergo further fractionation to produce andesites and dacites (Section 3.4.2). Furthermore, the bulk partition coefficients of compatible elements can be obtained from log–log plots of the data, and these can be used to calculate the mineralogical make-up of the fractionating mineral assemblage (Section 3.4.3).

3.4.4 Rare earth element geochemistry

Trace element abundances, and in particular the differences in abundances of a given trace element can tell us a lot about the chemical processes in magmas. The information that we can extract includes the mineralogy, proportions and absolute amounts of fractionating crystals. One group of trace elements has a particular interest—the **rare earth elements**, or **REE** for short. They are often used to investigate geochemical processes, as you will find here and in some later parts of this Course.

The REE have atomic numbers between 57 and 71 (Table 3.5) and have common chemical properties. For instance they all form trivalent ions (although Eu forms Eu^{2+} as well as Eu^{3+}) and they have ionic radii in the restricted range 103.2 pm to 86.1 pm (picometres). REE with low atomic numbers (and therefore low atomic mass) are referred to as **light REE**, or **LREE**, whilst those with high atomic mass are **heavy REE**, or **HREE**.

Table 3.5 Ionic radii for trivalent rare earth elements (REE) and normalizing chondritic REE abundances

Atomic number	Element	Symbol	Ionic radius/pm	Chondritic abundance normalizing values/p.p.m.
57	lanthanum	La	103.2	0.367
58	cerium	Ce	101	0.957
59	praseodymium	Pr	99	0.137
60	neodymium	Nd	98.3	0.711
61	promethium	Pm	*	*
62	samarium	Sm	95.8	0.231
63	europium	Eu	94.7	0.087
64	gadolinium	Gd	93.8	0.306
65	terbium	Tb	92.3	0.058
66	dysprosium	Dy	91.2	0.381
67	holmium	Ho	90.1	0.0851
68	erbium	Er	89.0	0.249
69	thulium	Tm	88.0	0.0356
70	ytterbium	Yb	86.8	0.248
71	lutetium	Lu	86.1	0.0381

*Pm has no stable isotopes and does not occur in nature.

Concentrations of REE are reported in parts per million (p.p.m.), just like any other trace element, but are often displayed graphically after being normalized to (divided by) the REE concentrations of chondritic meteorites (Figure 3.22). The reason for this normalization is to get round the fact that REE with even atomic numbers are more abundant than those with odd atomic numbers (see Table 3.5). By normalizing the data, the 'spiky' nature of the REE abundances are removed and replaced by a smooth pattern (Figure 3.22) whose regularity brings out the geochemical coherence of this group of elements. The straight lines connecting individual chondrite-normalized points define the **REE pattern** of each rock. Thus the REE pattern of chondrites would be a horizontal line with a y-axis value of 1.0. Most rocks have higher REE abundances and so plot above that line—for example the Santorini lavas in Figure 3.22.

What can be learnt from REE patterns? What do they tell us about magmatic processes?

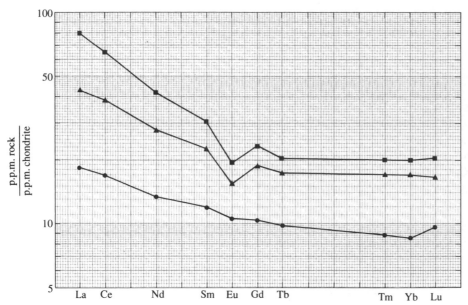

Figure 3.22 Chondrite-normalized REE patterns of Santorini basalt (circles), basaltic andesite (triangles) and andesite (squares).

Look first at just one element, say La, and how it varies from the basalt to the andesite at Santorini.

Is La an incompatible or compatible trace element in the Santorini magmas?

The concentration in the most silicic rock is higher than that in the less silicic rocks, so, like Th, La must be an incompatible trace element.

All the REE are behaving incompatibly, and this is because their K_D values for most minerals are less than 1. For example, partition coefficients in basalts and andesites are shown in Figure 3.23 to be less than 1 except for the HREE in garnet. Notice that for each mineral, K_D varies fairly systematically from LREE to HREE (with the exception of europium, Eu), with the HREE tending to have the largest partition coefficients. When the LREE become enriched during fractional crystallization, the HREE will be only moderately enriched (as at Santorini) or even depleted if garnet is crystallizing and causes $D_{HREE} > 1$.

There are three aspects of REE patterns such as Figure 3.22 that are especially useful in studies of magma fractionation:

1   The slope of the pattern (positive or negative slope).
2   The steepness of the slope.
3   The nature of the perturbation in each pattern shown by europium (Eu).

Points 1 and 2 have already been mentioned; fractional crystallization will generally cause the LREE to become enriched more rapidly than HREE so that the REE pattern has a negative slope. The steepness of the slope depends on the amount of crystals removed by fractionation and the partition coefficients of the fractionating crystal assemblage. (The complementary cumulate rocks will have lower abundances of REE and show REE patterns with shallower slopes.)

One way of describing the steepness of a REE pattern is to calculate the ratio of LREE to HREE. Specifically, the ratio of the normalized abundance of La or Ce to that of Yb or Lu is used for this purpose. We shall consider the elements Ce and Yb, and the ratio $(Ce/Yb)_N$ where the subscript N is there to remind us that we are dealing with chondrite-normalized abundances.

ITQ 3.16   What is $(Ce/Yb)_N$ for (a) the basalt in Figure 3.22 (b) the andesite in Figure 3.22 (remember that the vertical axis has a logarithmic scale).

The andesite's REE pattern certainly looks to be the steepest on Figure 3.22, and the calculation of $(Ce/Yb)_N$ confirms this. To see how $(Ce/Yb)_N$ changes during fractionation of Santorini's magmas, this ratio has to be plotted against some index of fractionation such as SiO_2, MgO or Th. Since Th was identified as the most incompatible element in Section 3.4.2, Th is the most natural choice as it will show

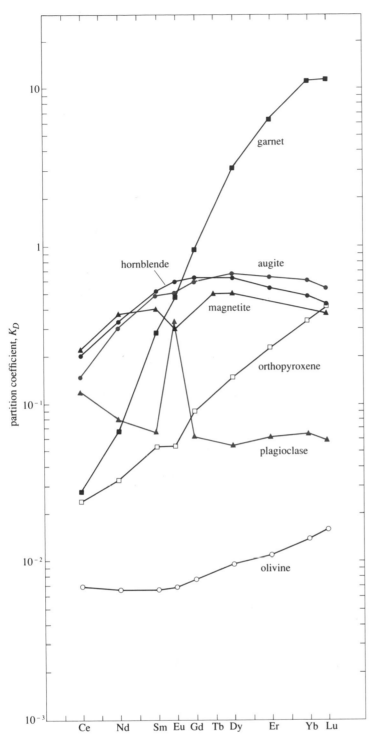

Figure 3.23 Partition coefficients (K_D) of selected REE between minerals and basic magma.

maximum variation. Figure 3.24 shows that $(Ce/Yb)_N$ increases slightly as Th rises to about 10 p.p.m., and thereafter $(Ce/Yb)_N$ increases more rapidly. Thus Ce becomes enriched by fractional crystallization more rapidly than does Yb in Santorini's magmas. This is especially so in the andesites and dacites with more than about 10 p.p.m. Th. Doesn't this sound familiar? We found earlier (Section 3.4.2) that the change from a plagioclase + augite + olivine mineralogy to plagioclase + augite + orthopyroxene + magnetite mineralogy at *c.* 10 p.p.m. Th (*c.* 55% SiO_2) caused the bulk partition coefficients of several trace elements to change, leading to fractionation trends with kinks in them at *c.* 10 p.p.m. Th. The steepness of the REE patterns is thus reflecting the same controls on trace element fractionation behaviour.

Returning to Figure 3.22, each lava has a fairly smooth REE pattern except for the odd behaviour of europium in the basaltic andesite and andesite. These magmas fractionated from the basalt, but clearly Eu has not been enriched as much as the neighbouring elements samarium (Sm) and gadolinium (Gd).

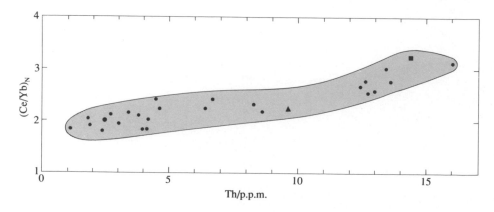

Figure 3.24 Plot of $(Ce/Yb)_N$ against Th for Santorini lavas. The circle, triangle and square identify the basalt, basaltic andesite and andesite whose REE patterns are given in Figure 3.22.

ITQ 3.17 Which mineral will provide Eu with an anomalous fractionation behaviour? (Hint: think about the K_D values for Eu).

Europium has an anomalously high K_D value for plagioclase because it occurs as Eu^{2+}, enabling it to enter the Ca^{2+} site in the plagioclase structure (just as Sr^{2+} does: recall that $K_{Sr}^{plag/liq} > 1$, e.g. Table 3.4), whereas Sm^{3+} and Gd^{3+} cannot and are, therefore, much more incompatible. The spike at Eu in the values of partition coefficients for plagioclase (Figure 3.23) will be reflected by a trough in the REE patterns of lavas that have been formed by fractionation of a plagioclase-bearing assemblage. The extracted plagioclase-bearing cumulate will be correspondingly rich in Eu and its REE pattern will have a spike at Eu. When plagioclase has not been involved, the REE pattern will not show a perturbation at Eu. Thus the unusual, or anomalous, behaviour of Eu is a very useful indicator of the role of plagioclase fractionation or accumulation in a rock's genesis.

The perturbation, either a spike or a trough, is known as the **europium anomaly**. A spike, reflecting plagioclase accumulation, is called a positive europium anomaly and a trough, reflecting plagioclase removal, is a negative europium anomaly.

A simple way of describing the size of an europium anomaly is illustrated in Figure 3.25, which shows the REE pattern of a rhyolite with a negative europium anomaly. The REE pattern is smooth, and if Eu hadn't been one of the analysed elements, we would anticipate Eu to plot at a value identified as Eu* ($=21.8$), which lies on the straight line joining Sm with Gd. The real value (10.3) departs from this interpolated concentration, of course, such that the europium anomaly can be given as

$$Eu/Eu* = 10.3/21.8 = 0.47$$

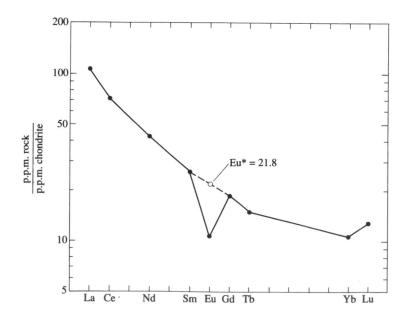

Figure 3.25 The REE pattern of a rhyolite, showing the method of finding Eu* needed to calculate the europium anomaly Eu/Eu*.

ITQ 3.18 What is the europium anomaly of (a) the basalt, (b) the basaltic andesite, and (c) the andesite from Santorini whose REE patterns are given in Figure 3.22.

ITQ 3.19 What does your answer to ITQ 3.18 imply about the relative amounts of plagioclase fractionation involved in generating the basaltic andesite and the andesite from the basalt?

If you still need convincing that plagioclase is an important fractionating mineral at Santorini, then Figure 3.26 reinforces the observation from Figure 3.22 that the negative europium anomaly becomes more pronounced as fractionation continues. Subduction zone magmas in general show negative Eu anomalies, reflecting the importance of plagioclase—an abundant phenocryst phase in all but the most magnesian rocks.

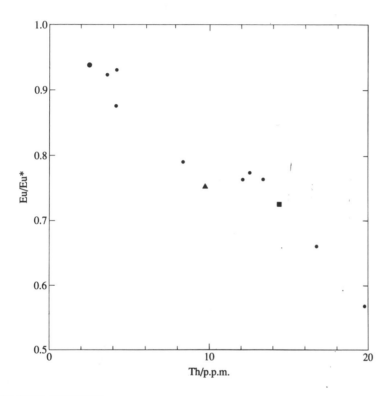

Figure 3.26 Plot of the europium anomaly Eu/Eu* against Th for Santorini lavas. The circle, triangle and square identify the basalt, basaltic andesite and andesite whose REE patterns are given in Figure 3.22.

3.5 MAGMA MIXING

The rocks we have studied so far were shown to be related by fractional crystallization. However, not all of the magmas erupted from Santorini (and most other volcanoes for that matter) were formed by fractional crystallization. For example, look at Plate 3.2 in the CPB, which shows a pumice from the Minoan eruption. This piece of pumice is dominantly a white, dacitic rock (68% SiO_2 in this case). Dark streaks and blotches are also to be seen, and these are andesitic in composition (here, 58% SiO_2). A thin section of a similar pumice (Plate 3.3 in the CPB) shows that the contact between the two components is sharp but complex, as if the andesitic liquid was being stirred into the dacite. This is in fact just what has happened—the pumice is a frozen specimen of a streaky mixture of two liquid magmas. The sharp contacts between the different glasses indicate that the stirring process must have been interrupted at the instant of the eruption in order for such fine and delicate structures to be preserved. Pumices such as those of Plates 3.2 and 3.3 in the CPB are by no means rare, and are often referred to as **streaky pumice** or **banded pumice** because of their distinctive appearance. The overall, or bulk, composition of the banded pumice in Plate 3.2 must be between 58 and 68% SiO_2. The constituent parts, andesite and dacite, may have formed by fractional crystallization, but the resultant mixture has formed by a different process, that of **magma mixing**. As its name implies, magma mixing is a process that causes two (or more) magmas to become mingled together, forming a new magma of an intermediary composition. The two magmas may come together when one is injected into the base of a magma chamber which contains the other magma (Figure 3.27a). The arrival of the new magma will cause the chamber pressure to rise, and the overlying ground surface will swell. Meanwhile, the two magmas can start to become mixed together by convection and turbulence in the chamber (Figure 3.27b). Then if sufficient magma has entered the chamber, the country rock will break and some of the chamber's contents will be erupted (Figure 3.27c). The eruption products will comprise mixed magmas, such as the banded pumice of Plate 3.2. The streaky nature of such pumice is a plain illustration of the processes sketched in Figure 3.27. However, in other cases, the stirring action within the chamber may be more effective, and so produce a homogeneous blend of the two magmas. Thus it may take more than visual inspection to recognize the hybrid nature of such magmas. Moreover, since the recharge of magma chambers can commonly trigger eruptions it is of some concern to be able to identify the frequency of magma mixing events in a volcano's history. Compositional and petrographic studies are used to identify mixed magmas in ways that are described next. Within the Skaros lava sequence, there are a number of mixed magmas that illustrate the key points.

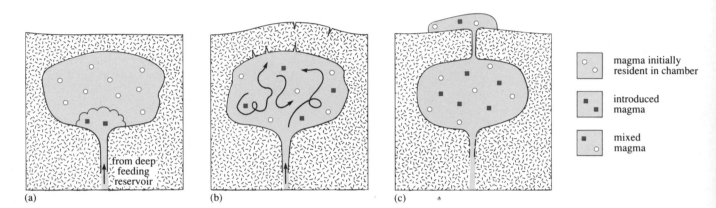

Figure 3.27 Cartoon of the addition of magma into the base of a pre-existing magma chamber. (a) Injection of new magma. (b) Pressure within the replenished chamber builds up, deforming the overburden. Turbulence in the chamber leads to the two magmas becoming mixed together. (c) Pressure is released by the escape of mixed magma in an eruption when the replenished chamber bursts open.

3.5.1 Magma mixing revealed by chemical composition

The easiest way of appreciating the compositional traits of a set of rocks is often to draw a variation diagram. In Section 3.4, we found that the easiest way to identify fractional crystallization was with a graphical test. A straight line trend on a log–log graph of a compatible trace element plotted against an incompatible trace element indicated the operation of the fractional crystallization process within a rock series. Can we obtain a similar type of graphical test to identify the magma mixing process?

Consider two magmas (A and B) which have different compositions. If some of B is mixed into A to create a new mixed magma, C, then on linear graph paper, a plot of one element against another will show C plotting on the straight line that joins A and B (Figure 3.28). Magma C is said to contain the two **end-member magmas** A and B. If the mixing process is relatively inefficient and produces a series of blends, with different proportions of the end members, then this range of mixed magma compositions will plot as an array of points on the mixing line AB (Figure 3.28). A straight line trend on linear graph paper is thus indicative of magma mixing.

The chemical evidence of magma mixing is best sought from a plot, on linear graph paper, of an incompatible trace element against a compatible trace element. As an example, consider the variation between Ni and Rb, which we studied when developing our ideas about Rayleigh fractionation. Figure 3.29 reproduces Figure 3.18a and identifies two magmas labelled A and B. Magma B has been derived by fractional crystallization of magma A, so both lie on the *curved* fractionation trend. Mixtures of A and B will lie on the *straight* mixing line which plots above the

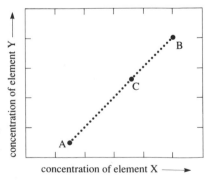

Figure 3.28 Variation diagram showing the concentrations of two elements (X and Y) in two magmas (A and B) and the compositions of various mixtures of A and B, including one labelled C. Note linear scale on axes.

fractionation trend. For example, mixed magma C contains over 20 p.p.m. more Ni than a fractionated magma with the same Rb content. In general, *mixed magmas generated from end members that lie on a fractionation trend have unexpectedly high compatible element contents*. This is a distinctive chemical property which can be used to distinguish mixed magmas from fractionated magmas.

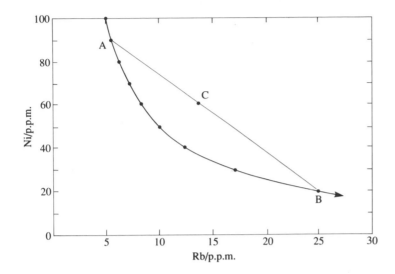

Figure 3.29 Plot of Ni against Rb showing the curved fractionation trend (black) of Figure 3.18a which gives rise to magmas A and B. Mixtures of A and B, such as C, lie on the mixing trend (red), and this trend lies above the fractionation trend.

We thus have two techniques for identifying mixed magmas on the basis of their chemical composition.

1   A suite of mixed magmas formed by mixing the same two end members in different proportions will plot on a straight line on all element versus element variation diagrams plotted on linear graph paper. The compositions of the end members define the end-points of the mixing line.

2   A mixed magma formed by mixing two end members that are related by fractional crystallization will be enriched in compatible elements. In other words, on a plot of a compatible element (e.g. Ni) against an incompatible element (e.g. Rb or Th) a mixed magma will plot above the curve defined by a fractionation trend (e.g. Figure 3.29).

So far, all of the Skaros lavas we have dealt with fall close to fractionation trends (Figures 3.19 and 3.20) and can thus be accounted for by fractional crystallization. However, there are a further eight Skaros lavas, which are introduced now for the first time, and these do not conform to the fractionation trends. As seen in Figure 3.30, these eight lavas plot above the trend followed by those magmas at Santorini that formed by fractional crystallization.

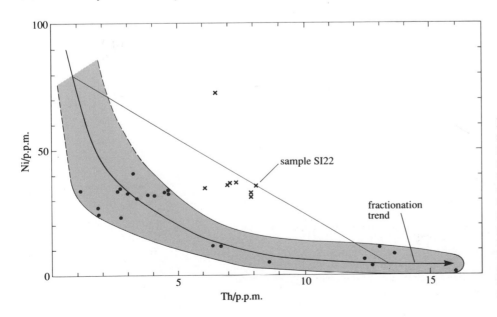

Figure 3.30 Plot of Ni against Th, showing the field enclosing magmas from Santorini that formed by fractional crystallization, including those from Skaros (points). The path of the fractionation trend is labelled. Crosses identify the mixed magmas from Skaros. These magmas can be accounted for by the mixing of two members of the fractionation series. A mixing line (in red) illustrates one combination that can produce the mixed magma labelled 'sample SI22' (cf. Figure 3.29).

3.5.2 Mineralogy of mixed magmas

Just as the chemical composition of a mixed magma reflects the composition of the end members, so its mineralogy will be inherited from the mineralogy of its end members. Thus, mixing of two phenocryst-bearing magmas will generate a mixed magma with a complicated but distinctive mineralogy. The compositions and textures of the various minerals provide another means of identifying mixed magmas. We can also use the mineralogy to discover the nature of the end-member magmas. To illustrate how this can be done, we shall consider one of the mixed magmas from Skaros, (sample number SI22 plotted on Figure 3.30), which contains crystals of plagioclase, augite, orthopyroxene, olivine and magnetite. How can this assemblage arise by the mixing of two magmas? In Section 3.3.2, we found that the Skaros magmas produced by fractional crystallization can be divided into two types on the basis of their mineralogy (Figure 3.11). Those containing olivine generally have less than about 55% SiO_2, and those containing orthopyroxene and magnetite generally have more than about 55% SiO_2.

> **ITQ 3.20**   What conclusions can you now draw about the compositions of the end-member magmas involved in the genesis of SI22?

So, the mineral assemblage tells us something about the nature of the end members. We can get more information from the compositions of the minerals themselves, however.

We also found in Section 3.3.2 that the composition of phenocrysts that are in chemical equilibrium with their host magma will reflect the composition of that magma. For example, a magma with a low MgO content, such as dacite, will precipitate augite with a lower Mg ratio than that grown from a high-MgO magma, such as basalt (Figure 3.14 and Figure 3.31a). If these two magmas become mixed together (Figure 3.31b), then the two types of augite crystals get stirred together and the liquid portions of the magmas become blended to form a new liquid. This new liquid will not be in chemical equilibrium with either of the pre-existing augite crystals and these disequilibrium crystals are called **xenocrysts**. The xenocrysts become overgrown by augite that is in chemical equilibrium with the new mixed liquid (Figure 3.31b). Similar effects occur with olivine and plagioclase crystals. Thus the compositions of the cores of crystals tell us about the composition of the magmas from which they grew prior to mixing, while the outermost parts of the crystals have compositions that are related to the composition of the liquid formed by mixing.

This sequence of crystal growth, mixing and further crystal growth illustrated in Figures 3.31a and 3.31b can be worked out from observations of mixed magmas such as SI22 from Skaros. Here, of course, we start with the final product of these processes and have to work backwards to find the compositions of the two end members that became mixed.

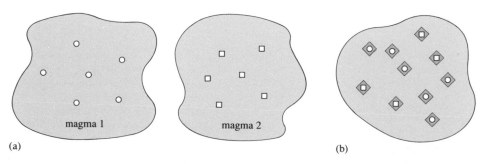

(a)   (b)

Figure 3.31   (a) Two separate magmas with different compositions contain augite crystals with different compositions (illustrated here schematically by different shapes). (b) When the magmas in (a) are mixed together, a mixed magma is formed that inherits both augite types, and these crystals become overgrown by augite whose composition is in chemical equilibrium with the enclosing mixed liquid. The rims of all the augite crystals (shown in red) then share the same composition, but there are two kinds of core composition.

ITQ 3.21 Dr. J. P. P. Huijsmans of Utrecht University used the electron microprobe to find that the cores of augite crystals in SI22 have compositions of either $En_{47}Fs_9Wo_{44}$ or $En_{43}Fs_{18}Wo_{39}$. He also found the olivines to have cores of Fo_{87} while plagioclase crystals have cores of either $An_{88\ to\ 73}$ or $An_{65\ to\ 52}$.

(a) Calculate the Mg ratios of the augite cores and use your answer, with Figure 3.14, to estimate the MgO contents of the end-member magmas in SI22.

(b) Estimate the MgO content of the end member from which the olivine grew (using Figure 3.12).

(c) Estimate the SiO_2 contents of the end members using the plagioclase core compositions in SI22 and the observations reported in Table 3.2, Section 3.3.2.

How does this fit with the chemical composition of SI22 itself? SI22 should fall on a mixing line between the two end members you identified in answering ITQ 3.21. These end members can be recognized on a variation diagram such as Figure 3.32. Assuming that they belong to the series of fractionated magmas, then the compositions you found in ITQ 3.21 must be close to 7% MgO, 60 to 70 p.p.m. Ni and 3% MgO, 5 to 10 p.p.m. Ni. As Figure 3.32 shows, they can be combined to yield a mixed magma with the same composition as SI22.

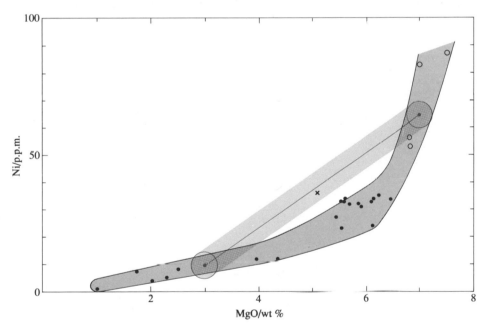

Figure 3.32 Plot of Ni against MgO, showing the compositions of lavas from Skaros (points) and elsewhere on Santorini (open circles) that are related by fractional crystallization, together with the approximate compositions of two end members (red points) whose chemical and mineralogical compositions can account for the mixed magma sample SI22 (the cross).

So, the chemical and mineralogical compositions of SI22 have allowed us to identify it as a mixed magma and to identify the end members from which it formed. In fact, from this one rock we have managed to learn about two magmas! One of the end members is otherwise unknown at Skaros as there are no basaltic flows with more than 6.5% MgO or 41 p.p.m. Ni in the lava pile. This provides evidence for the existence of more primitive high-Ni basalt which is not erupted at Skaros but which is similar to other Santorini basalts.

We have seen how information about the early stages in the genesis of a mixed magma is contained in the cores of the crystals. The later stages of the mixing process are recorded by the outermost parts of these crystals and by the microphenocrysts which grew in the groundmass of the lava at the time of its eruption. These minerals grew while thermal and chemical equilibrium was being re-attained after mixing had taken place. Since the composition of the mixed magma is intermediate between those of the end members, the compositions of the crystals that grow from this mixture will similarly be intermediate between those which precipitated from the end members. Thus, in SI22, the rims of all the augites have similar compositions (around $En_{45}Fs_{12}Wo_{43}$) and the rims of all the plagioclase have similar compositions (in the range An_{70} to An_{62}) reflecting crystallization from a single melt composition intermediate between those that precipitated the two core populations. The microphenocrysts in the groundmass share their compositions with the rims of the larger crystals and must have grown from the same liquid that was in equilibrium with the phenocryst rims.

Textural evidence in thin section for magma mixing is most spectacularly shown by plagioclase crystals (Figure 3.33a). When sodic plagioclase is brought into contact with a hotter calcic magma, the feldspar starts to partially melt. The edges of the crystal become corroded, developing an intricate sponge-like or **sieve texture** (Figure 3.33b) that consists of dark glass and clear feldspar. Plainly this crystal was far from being in equilibrium with its host. However, the crystal has become overgrown by a rim of clear feldspar precipitated from the liquid generated by magma mixing. This jacket of equilibrium feldspar protects the interior of the crystal locking in the textural evidence for a severe hiatus in the magma's evolution.

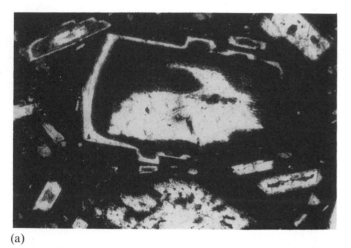

(a)   (b)

Figure 3.33 (a) Photomicrograph in plane-polarized light of a plagioclase crystal in a mixed magma, showing a dark zone, with rounded outline, caused by chemical attack during magma mixing. A clear feldspar rim encloses the crystal, and was formed by equilibrium growth from the host liquid after magma mixing had occurred. (Field of view is 2.7 mm long.) (b) Close-up of the corroded, sieve-textured, part of the feldspar crystal in (a) (Field of view is 0.225 mm long.)

Similar reactions affect pyroxene and olivine phenocrysts when they are involved in magma mixing. In general, this results in those crystals that have grown from a hot mafic end member (Mg-rich ferromagnesian minerals and Ca-rich feldspar) to retain straight crystal faces and become mantled by rims that show **normal zoning** (i.e. less Mg- or Ca-rich towards the margin). Meanwhile, Mg-poor ferromagnesian minerals and Ca-poor plagioclase from a more evolved, cooler, end member undergo partial melting (sieve-textures) and are overgrown by **reversely zoned** rims (i.e. more Mg- or Ca-rich towards the margin).

By carefully studying the rocks of Santorini, it has been possible to identify two processes that have controlled the evolution of this volcano's magmas. These are fractional crystallization and magma mixing, and are the consequences of heat loss from a shallow magma chamber and replenishment of this chamber by hot primitive magmas. These are fundamental aspects of magmatic plumbing systems and contribute to the petrology of igneous rocks above subduction zones.

3.6 MAGMATIC PROCESSES THROUGH TIME

To fully appreciate the workings of a simple subduction zone volcano such as Santorini, the compositional variation of the lavas needs to be seen in a stratigraphic sequence. The order of eruption of the Skaros magmas is neatly shown by the stratigraphy of the exposures in the caldera wall (Figure 3.6). The variation in SiO_2 and Th contents with stratigraphic position is shown in Figure 3.34. Crosses denote magmas formed by mixing and dots denote magmas derived by fractional crystallization (according to the criteria we studied in Sections 3.4 and 3.5). It is clear from Figure 3.34 that the magma composition fluctuated through time—there is no overall trend toward more evolved or more primitive compositions with time. A further point that emerges is that the mixed magmas were erupted mainly in two periods rather than being scattered throughout the sequence. These observations tell of the competition between fractionation, eruption and mixing rates at the volcano. For example, if fractionation is rapid and efficient, then successive eruptions will be of progressively more evolved magmas. This could explain the origin of the sequences labelled A in Figure 3.34.

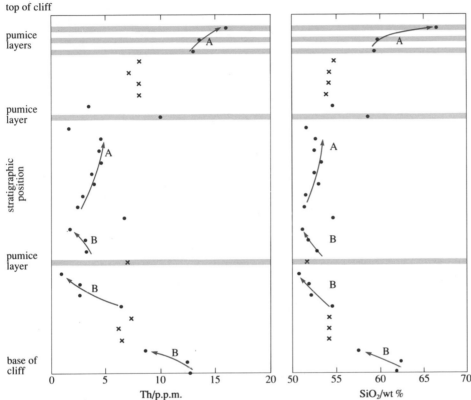

Figure 3.34 Composition of magmas shown in stratigraphic sequence from the base of the Skaros cliff to the capping layers of pumice. Points denote fractionated magmas; crosses denote mixed magmas. Sequences of eruptions labelled A become more evolved with time, those labelled B become less evolved with time.

To look into this further, it is necessary to find out how fractional crystallization may operate. Left to cool down, a magma chamber will start to solidify as crystals grow on the chamber walls and in the convecting magma itself. Fractionated magmas can then be produced by the settling out of these crystals. This is probably not a very efficient process, however, because the density of plagioclase is close to that of andesitic magma, so there will always be some phenocrysts left suspended in the magma. This may be one reason why subduction zone andesites are characteristically rich in plagioclase. Certainly the complex zoning patterns in some of the phenocrysts record a lengthy history of crystal growth within the chamber (cf. Plate 3.1 CPB).

It is probable that magmatic evolution processes occur near the chamber's margins rather than within its interior. Crystallization at the chamber walls must produce a fractionated liquid. This liquid has a different composition and temperature from the warmer magma in the interior of the chamber and will therefore have a different density. The fractionated liquid will either float upwards, accumulating at the chamber roof, or sink downwards, accumulating at the chamber floor. To work out how the magma will behave we need to know how density is related to composition and temperature. We will keep thinks simple and only deal with liquids, ignoring the influence of suspended crystals.

Like most substances magma contracts when it cools; its density increases by 0.02×10^3 kg m^{-3} for every 100 °C drop in temperature. The compositional changes caused by fractionation are generally much more significant than the accompanying fall in temperature, however. As you might expect, the amount of iron in a magma has a marked influence on its density, with iron-rich magmas being denser than iron-poor magmas.

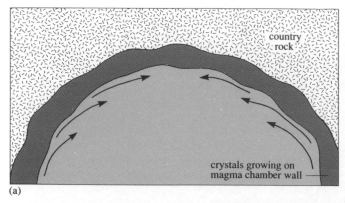

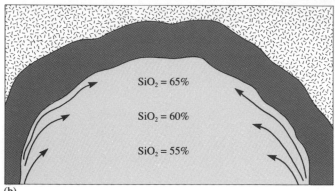

Will a fractionated calc-alkaline magma be more dense or less dense than its parent?

Fractional crystallization of calc-alkaline basalt leads to a series of magmas with progressively lower FeO_t contents, as the analyses in Table 3.1 show. Similarly, calc-alkaline magmas do not show an iron-enrichment trend on the AFM diagram (Figure 3.10). Thus calc-alkaline dacite will be less dense than andesite, which will in turn be less dense than basalt.

Consequently, the fractionated liquids that are produced when crystals grow on the walls of a magma chamber will have low densities and rise towards the chamber roof (Figure 3.35a). This physical process is called **convective fractionation** as it involves convection (i.e. motion driven by density differences) of fractionated magmas. Convective fractionation is believed to be an important process in calc-alkaline magma chambers like the one beneath Santorini. In particular, it exerts three major influences over the evolution of magma chambers and thus on the compositions of erupted magmas:

1   With time, the volume of fractionated magma which accumulates in the roof of the chamber will increase.

2   A range of fractionated compositions will develop in such a way that the chamber becomes vertically zoned in terms of composition and temperature. The lightest magma (which will be the most fractionated and, therefore, coolest magma) will occupy the very top of the chamber and grade downwards to denser more mafic compositions (Figures 3.35b and c). Such a chamber is said to possess compositional zonation or to be compositionally zoned, i.e. it is a **zoned magma chamber**.

3   The most fractionated, uppermost, magma in the chamber will become more evolved with time.

The above points can help in understanding the magmatic history represented by the Skaros lava sequence of Figure 3.34.

Let us assume that the magma chamber has evolved to the state where andesites grade downward to basaltic andesites. When the top of this zoned chamber is sampled by a series of eruptions, the successive lavas will tap progressively deeper parts of the chamber. This results in a sequence of lavas that become more mafic upwards through the succession such as the sequences labelled B in Figure 3.34. During these periods, fractionation appears to have been slow enough (or the

Figure 3.35   (a) Sketch of the roof zone of a magma chamber indicating the rise of fractionated liquids from crystals growing on the margins of the chamber (i.e. convective fractionation).
(b) Sketch illustrating a compositional gradient created by convective fractionation in the roof of a magma chamber.
(c) Photograph of a laboratory model of convective fractionation in a magma chamber. A solution of sodium carbonate has become saturated on the cold pitched walls of the chamber, leading to crystallization and the release of chemically fractionated (i.e. dilute) sodium carbonate solution. The fractionated magmas have formed a compositionally zoned region occupying the top third of the chamber (cf. Figure 3.35b). Settled crystals are also growing on the floor of the chamber. Total height of laboratory chamber is 30 cm. (See video VC 272: *Island Arc Magmatism: Santorini* and its accompanying video notes for further information about this laboratory model.)

eruption rate was sufficiently frequent) to prevent evolved magmas from being regenerated during the intervals between eruptions. In contrast, when the fractionation rate outpaces the eruption rate, successive eruptions are of more evolved magmas, as we already noted for the sequences labelled A in Figure 3.34.

Lastly, the sequences of mixed magmas (Figure 3.34) are likely to reflect times of heightened rates of chamber replenishment by batches of new primitive magmas. The overall Skaros sequence displays episodes of advancing fractionation, exhaustion of a zoned magma chamber and mixing between resident and incoming magmas.

In eruptions of large volume, such as those associated with caldera formation, several levels of a zoned magma chamber can be erupted. This appears to have been what happened in the Minoan eruption at Santorini. In this eruption, compositions range from 68 to 58% SiO_2. This devastating event post-dated the previous known eruption by about 14 000 years. This long time gap (intervals between most other eruptions at Santorini are measured in tens or hundreds of years) seems to have been long enough for a large volume of compositionally zoned magma to build up in the magma chamber. When the pressure in the chamber was released, about 20 km^3 of magma was erupted, destroying much of the volcano and obliterating the township of Akrotiri. The volcanology of the Minoan eruption, its relationships to the rest of Santorini, and the models of magmatic evolution are drawn together in the video programme VC272 *Island-Arc Magmatism: Santorini*, which you should now watch; the running time is 38 minutes.

Summary

1   Santorini, in the Aegean arc, is a well-studied example of an island arc volcano. It has had a varied eruptive history including andesitic lava flows that have built up about four overlapping shield volcanoes such as the Skaros shield. Dacitic lava domes and pumice eruptions have also occurred. The latter have often been of sufficient volume to create collapse calderas that allowed the sea to enter the centre of the volcano giving Santorini its present topography and shoreline. The most recent caldera-forming eruption was the Minoan eruption and took place *c*. 3 500 years ago. It produced widespread pumice beds, including pyroclastic flow deposits, that blanket the island and adjacent sea floor and destroyed Minoan habitations. Younger eruptions have started to rebuild the volcano.

2   The chemical compositions of Santorini's lavas and ashes illustrate the geochemistry of subduction zone volcanoes. The important plots are of K_2O versus SiO_2 (Figure 3.8), FeO_t/MgO versus SiO_2 (Figure 3.9) and the AFM triangular diagram (Figure 3.10). Subduction zone magmas cover a continuous range from basalt through basaltic andesite, andesite, dacite and sometimes rhyolite, with the different rock types being defined on the basis of SiO_2 content (Figure 3.8). Individual volcanoes, or even arcs, produce magma series that can be classed as either low-K, medium-K or high-K (Figure 3.8). Also, those magma series in which FeO_t/MgO of basalt and basaltic andesite increases rapidly as SiO_2 increases fall into the field of tholeiitic magmas (Figure 3.9) while those with lower and less variable FeO_t/MgO are calc-alkaline. Likewise, tholeiitic series show an arched trend of iron enrichment on an AFM diagram, while calc-alkaline series show minor or negligible iron enrichment (Figure 3.10). Like most subduction zone volcanoes Santorini has a calc-alkaline (medium-K) magma series. Certain arcs, notably those on oceanic crust in island arcs (e.g. Tonga, Mariana) are tholeiitic (low-K).

3   The chemical compositions of igneous minerals correlate with the composition of their host magma. Thus, ferromagnesian minerals grown from basalt are richer in Mg end-members (Fo in olivine, En in pyroxenes) than those in less magnesian magmas such as andesite and dacite. The Mg ratio, Mg/(Mg + Fe), of these minerals decreases as the MgO content of the host rock decreases. In parallel, the more primitive magmas have Ca-rich (An-rich) plagioclase feldspar, while andesites and dacites have progressively more sodic (An-poor, Ab-rich) plagioclase.

4   Trace element variation in a magma series can be investigated in terms of magmatic processes using the Rayleigh fractionation equation, which describes the effect of fractional crystallization on the concentration of a trace element:

$C_l = C_o F^{D-1}$ (equation 3.7). Incompatible trace elements (those with $D < 1$) therefore increase in concentration with fractionation (decreasing amount of remaining liquid, F) and compatible trace elements ($D > 1$) decrease in concentration.

When the concentrations of a highly compatible trace element are plotted against those of a highly incompatible trace element on log–log graph paper, a reasonable straight-line trend will be revealed only if fractional crystallization of a common parental magma is responsible for a magma series.

When the compatible element (with bulk partition coefficient $D_{compatible}$) is plotted on the vertical axis and the incompatible element (with $D_{incompatible}$) on the horizontal axis, the straight-line fractionation trend will have a negative trend with slope $m = (D_{compatible} - 1)/(D_{incompatible} - 1)$ (cf. equation 3.12). For a highly incompatible element, such as Th, $D_{incompatible} \approx 0$, so that by measuring the slope m on a log–log plot allows $D_{compatible}$ to be worked out. This bulk partition coefficient is essentially determined by the relative abundances and mineral partition coefficients, K_D, of the one or two minerals in the fractionating assemblage that have high K_D. For example, Sr is controlled almost entirely by plagioclase. It therefore becomes possible to determine the identity and proportions of fractionating minerals. At Santorini, and other arc volcanoes, plagioclase is dominant (50–60%), and this reflects its abundance in the modes of arc magmas. Basalts and basaltic andesites fractionate, in order of decreasing abundance, plagioclase, augite and olivine. More evolved magmas fractionate plagioclase, augite, orthopyroxene and magnetite.

5 Rare earth element (REE) patterns for arc magmas have negative slopes (e.g. $(Ce/Yb)_N > 1$) that steepen with fractionation. The REE patterns have negative europium anomalies (Eu/Eu* < 1) that deepen with fractionation and these are a hallmark of plagioclase fractionation.

6 Mixed magmas, formed within magma chambers by the mingling of different magmas have compositions that lie on straight lines joining the compositions of their constituent end members when plotted on linear graph paper (Figure 3.28). They have higher concentrations of compatible trace elements when compared with fractionated magmas with the same incompatible trace element concentrations (Figures 3.29, 3.30).

Mixed magmas contain minerals inherited from the end-member magmas. They thus have complex mineralogies, such as two populations of plagioclase and augite crystals. They commonly show disequilibrium textures, such as corroded margins or sieve textures.

Mixed magmas most likely form when a magma chamber receives an injection of magma from beneath. This process can increase the pressure in the chamber and so trigger some eruptions (Figure 3.27).

7 Evolved calc-alkaline magmas contain less FeO_t than more primitive calc-alkaline magmas. Consequently, magma density decreases during fractionation. As a result, calc-alkaline magma chambers can evolve by convective fractionation whereby fractionated melts released from sites of crystal growth on the relatively cold walls of magma chambers float to the roof of the chamber (Figure 3.35). Over time, a thick layer of compositionally zoned magmas can accumulate at the apex of the chamber, with the most evolved (less dense) magma being at the very top. This process can account for the evolved and sometimes zoned nature of the magmas erupted from arc volcanoes after very long periods of dormancy.

8 Magma chambers beneath simple arc volcanoes such as Santorini can behave in complex manners. As well as evolving by fractional crystallization, they can receive inputs of magma that mix with that already in the chamber, and of course they lose magma in eruptions. The time (stratigraphic) sequence of magma compositions thus reflects the interplay between different rates of these magmatic processes. These are reflected in the pattern of volcanic activity—frequent effusive small volume eruptions of more primitive magma types and infrequent explosive large volume eruptions of gas-rich evolved magmas.

SAQS FOR SECTION 3

SAQ 3.1 State whether each of the following statements is true or false:

(a) Tholeiitic magma series show an iron enrichment trend.

(b) Medium-K magma series typically have tholeiitic compositional trends.

(c) The Mg ratio of ferromagnesian minerals in equilibrium with a magma decreases with fractionation of the magma.

(d) Fractionated calc-alkaline magmas have higher densities than their parental magmas.

SAQ 3.2 (a) Arrange the following clinopyroxene compositions in order of increasing Mg ratio

$$A: En_{42}Fs_{12}Wo_{46} \qquad B: En_{39}Fs_{14}Wo_{47} \qquad C: En_{45}Fs_9Wo_{46}$$

(b) Which of the above pyroxene compositions would you most likely find in a basalt?

SAQ 3.3 As a result of fractional crystallization beneath Santorini, basalt 181 (Table 3.1) produces a magma with the composition of rock sample 153 (Table 3.1).

(a) Assuming that $D_{Th} = 0$, what fraction by mass of the basalt will remain as liquid magma 153?

(b) Explain why it is safe to assume $D_{Th} = 0$ during the fractionation of many magmas.

SAQ 3.4 (a) Using Figure 3.20, and assuming $D_{Th} = 0$, determine the bulk partition coefficient for strontium, D_{Sr}, in the evolved (Th > 10 p.p.m.) magmas of Skaros.

(b) Explain why D_{Sr} is different in the more primitive magmas.

SAQ 3.5 Table 3.6 summarizes selected trace element analyses of lavas from an island arc volcano. Magma A is the most primitive.

(a) Select two trace elements that will allow you to test the data for evidence of fractional crystallization and magma mixing.

(b) Plot the concentrations of your chosen elements on Figures 3.36 and 3.37. Explain why magma A is the parent to all but two of the other magmas. Draw a smooth line or curve through the data points that represent fractionated magmas.

(c) Name the two samples that do not conform to your fractionation trend. If these formed by the mixing of two magmas that belong to the fractionated series, estimate the compositions of these end members.

(d) If you had access to hand specimens and thin sections of the rocks, what evidence would you look for to strengthen the idea that two of these lavas were mixed magmas?

(e) Consider the concentrations of Sr in the magmas. What is the bulk partition coefficient of Sr? Do the data suggest that plagioclase was present in the fractionating mineral assemblage and if so, in what approximate proportion? (You may need to refer to the Table of mineral partition coefficients, K_D, in Table 3.4.) What kind of Eu anomaly would you expect rock E to have?

Table 3.6 Concentrations (p.p.m.) of selected trace elements in a suite of lavas. For use with SAQ 3.5

Sample	A	B	C	D	E	F	G	H	I	J
Ni	175	20	35	10	3	4	11	72	75	18
Th	1.0	9.4	2.9	6.7	15	12	6.9	4.1	1.8	4.6
Rb	7	66	20	47	105	84	48	29	13	32
Sr	300	304	298	305	307	301	296	309	304	303

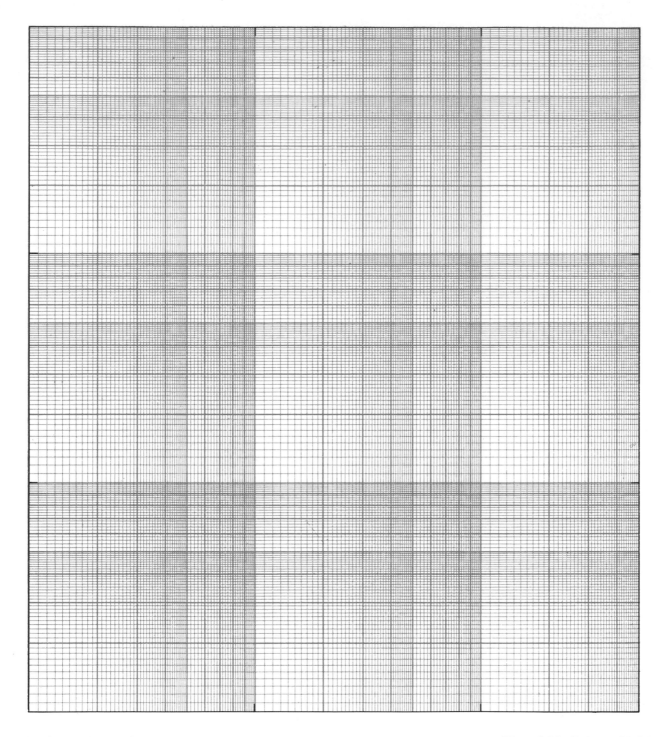

SAQ 3.6 State whether each of the following statements is true or false:

(a) The Aegean volcanic arc is about 150 km above a Benioff zone.

(b) Santorini was a large conical volcano prior to the caldera-forming Minoan eruption.

(c) Within the volcanic edifice of Santorini, magmas are often transported to the surface in NE–SW oriented dykes.

(d) At Santorini, hydrothermal systems are confined to the deepest parts of the caldera floor.

SAQ 3.7 (a) List, in stratigraphic order, the four major pyroclastic deposits that were produced by the Minoan eruption of Santorini.

(b) Why types of magma were erupted in the Minoan eruption?

(c) What is the approximate location of the vent of the Minoan eruption and how has it been inferred?

Figure 3.36 For use with SAQ 3.5.

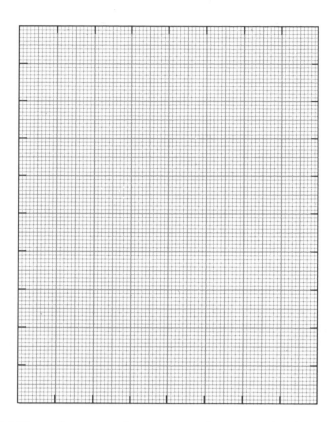

Figure 3.37 For use with SAQ 3.5.

SAQ 3.8 (a) Name the magmatic processes whose operation is revealed by the petrography and chemistry of Santorini's magmas.

(b) Briefly describe the key pieces of evidence that indicate the processes you have named in (a) to have operated.

(c) Briefly describe the process of convective fractionation as it occurs in calc-alkaline magma chambers.

4 SUBDUCTION ZONE MAGMATISM AT CONTINENTAL MARGINS

The evolution of continental crust can be influenced by inputs of mass and heat from subduction zone magmatism. In particular, the mass of the crust must be increased by the addition of mantle-derived arc magmas. In this Section, we start by examining geophysical information about the structure of both continental and oceanic crust that has been subjected to subduction zone magmatism. As well as comparing their crustal structures, we shall also ask whether the type and structure of the arc crust influences the nature of the erupted magmas. To answer this question, clues can be gathered from the volcanic rocks from the world's most notable active continental margin—the Andes. This volcanic region provides a natural laboratory in which to test new ideas and techniques for understanding magmatism at a continental margin.

4.1 CORRELATIONS BETWEEN CRUSTAL STRUCTURE AND MAGMA COMPOSITION

Subduction zones share many geological and geophysical traits (Figure 1.2), yet on a global scale they can display significant variations. The most obvious variation is in the twofold division into subduction zones that lie in ocean basins and those at the margins of continental crust. Is this just a simple topographic distinction between island arcs and continental margins, or are there more fundamental differences between oceanic and continental arcs? Obviously, normal oceanic and normal continental crusts are very different, but do these differences persist in crust that has been subjected to subduction zone processes? To answer these types of questions, we must compare the structures of the overriding plates in island arcs with those of active continental margins and also compare arc and non-arc crusts of oceanic and continental regions.

How might we carry out such comparisons?

Barring a costly very deep drilling project, it is impossible to sample the rocks throughout the entire thickness of the crust. To determine the nature of these inaccessible regions, we must rely on geophysical information. The results of seismic refraction surveys (Block 1B, Section 3.1) are of particular use here.

ITQ 4.1 What type of information about crustal structures and rock properties can be gained from seismic refraction studies?

Figure 4.1 summarizes the velocity structures in several volcanic arcs, and contrasts these with the velocity structure of continental and oceanic regions far from plate boundaries. You can pick out certain significant differences and similarities.

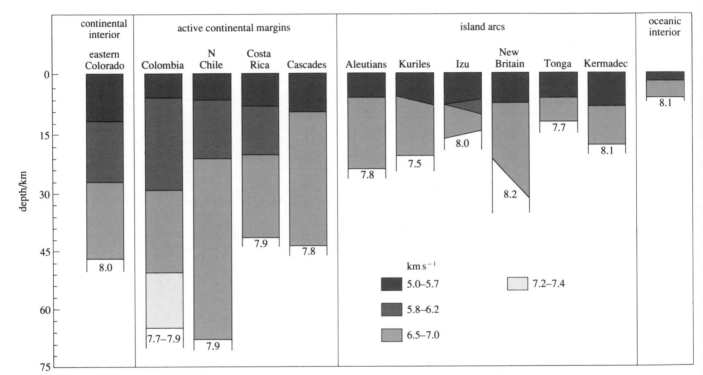

ITQ 4.2 (a) Is there a continuous range of P-wave velocities (v_p) present in the crustal sections shown in Figure 4.1?

(b) Briefly compare the absolute and relative thicknesses of the various seismic layers present in island arcs and in oceanic crust.

(c) Briefly compare the absolute and relative thicknesses of the various seismic layers present in active continental margins and in the continental interior.

(d) Briefly compare the crustal structures of active continental margins and island arcs.

(e) How do the seismic P-wave velocities of the uppermost mantle in volcanic arcs compare with those beneath normal oceanic and continental crust?

(f) Suggest an explanation for your answer to (e).

Figure 4.1 Crustal P-wave velocity structures of volcanic arcs, the continental interior and the oceanic interior. P-wave velocities (v_p in km s^{-1}) of the mantle immediately beneath the Moho are given at the bottom of each profile.

Your answers to ITQ 4.2 (b) and (c) should convince you that subduction-related processes have a significant influence on the crustal structure. For example, the roots of active continental margins can be considerably thicker than those of the continental interior, or shield, areas. Similarly, both the upper and lower layers of crust within island arcs are much thicker (by factors of between 2 and 6) than normal ocean crust. The most obvious conclusion is that magmatism has contributed to an increase in crustal thicknesses, i.e. material has been added to the crust as a result of subduction zone magmatism.

What processes affect magmas that enter arc crust?

Fractional crystallization and magma mixing are important processes that occur in magma chambers, and we studied these in Section 3.

You might expect that these processes will have more time to take effect when magma has to pass through thick continental crust than through thinner oceanic crust. If this is the case, then shouldn't there be some sort of correlation between the composition of the erupted magma and the structure of the underlying arc crust?

Indeed, as a *very broad generalization*, oceanic island arc volcanoes tend to erupt low-K (tholeiitic) basalts and basaltic andesites, whereas the volcanoes at active continental margins erupt a wider spectrum of medium-K (calc-alkaline) compositions ranging from basalt through to rhyolite. To explain this, some geologists have suggested that the thick continental margins provide more opportunities for magma to become lodged in the crust and therefore experience more fractionation, leading to increased proportions of dacite and rhyolite. Such a mechanism relies on the physical effects of the crustal structure and layering to govern the magmas' movement and compositional evolution. However, it cannot explain differences in the K_2O contents of parental basalts. Thus, a second group of geologists argue that to explain medium-K basalt in continental margins and low-K basalt in island arcs requires different degrees of partial melting or different mantle source compositions in the mantle wedges of these different types of subduction zone. (Their arguments are based on concepts you met in Block 2, Section 4). Yet another group feel that the somewhat higher SiO_2 and K_2O contents of the magmas at continental margins are due to melting and assimilation of pre-existing continental crust (which is relatively rich in SiO_2 and K_2O in comparison to basalt) into mantle-derived magmas; an effect known as **crustal contamination**. In other words, they favour a direct chemical influence of the crust on the composition of the magmas. No doubt all three ideas have their merits. However, since a magmatic process that we haven't considered before—crustal contamination—may play a role, we shall examine how this process can be identified and how it operates. To focus our exploration, the Andes are taken as a good place to study magmatism at an active continental margin.

4.2 NATURE OF THE SOUTH AMERICAN DESTRUCTIVE MARGIN

Subduction occurs along the entire 7 000 km length of western South America, where the Nazca and (in the extreme south) the Antarctic Plates descend beneath the South American Plate (TMOE, Figure 1.1). The Andean mountain chain lies parallel to the Peru–Chile Trench and is famed for its high volcanic peaks. It gives its name to andesite—the characteristic product of subduction zone magmatism. Superficially, the Andes represent the standard destructive plate margin, but this is very misleading, for the Andes display considerable variation in a number of features. Figures 4.2a–d show several geophysical and geological features of the Andean plate margin which bring this out.

> ITQ 4.3   Examine Figures 4.2a–d, and identify how the following parameters vary along the Andean plate margin:
>
> (a) presence of active volcanoes
>
> (b) dip angle of the Benioff zone
>
> (c) age and topography of ocean lithosphere entering the Peru–Chile trench
>
> (d) thickness of South American crust
>
> (e) age of South American basement

You should now be convinced that the nature of the subduction zone along the Andes is not constant. There are along-strike variations in the descending plate, the overriding plate and in the magmatic activity related to subduction. It is likely that at least some of these variations are related, and so the Andes offer the chance to look for these cause-and-effect relationships, and thereby discover how the subduction process operates. For instance, magmatism is absent where the Benioff zone has a shallow descent angle (Figure 4.2a and b), and these places coincide with

54

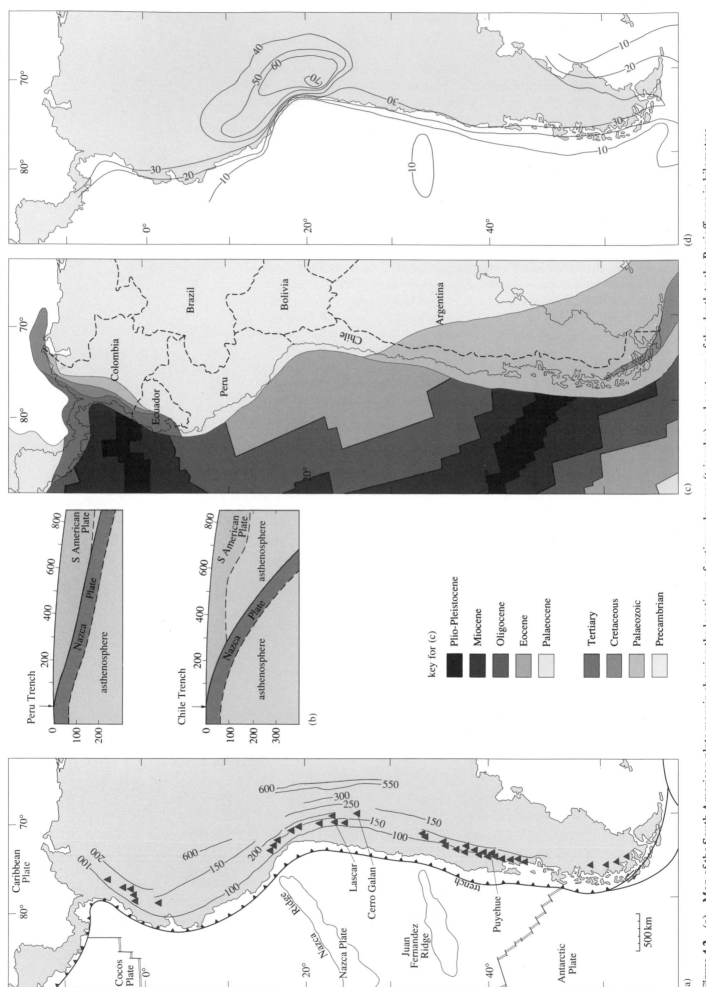

Figure 4.2 (a) Map of the South American plate margin showing the locations of active volcanoes (triangles) and contours of the depth to the Benioff zone in kilometres.
(b) Geometries of the Nazca and South American plates inferred from seismicity in central Peru and northern Chile. Horizontal distances are measured from the trench in kilometres.
(c) Map showing the ages of the South American basement and of the Nazca and Antarctic plates. (d) Map showing contours of crustal thickness in kilometres.

regions where basaltic seamount chains and aseismic ridges (i.e. the Juan Fernandez Ridge and Nazca Ridge) are entering the subduction zone (Figure 4.2a) or have done so within the last few million years. Why these striking correlations should exist remains obscure, but some people have argued that wherever upstanding seamounts are thrust into subduction zones, the upper basaltic layers are sheared off from the downgoing lithospheric plate. The remaining slab would, therefore, consist only of relatively dry peridotite. Without the wet basaltic layer, the downgoing slab would not have the raw materials to produce either amphibolite or eclogite. The implications of this are that first the slab would be insufficiently dense to sink at a steep angle and second the mantle wedge would not receive the water-rich fluids needed to induce partial melting.

Elsewhere in the Andes, subduction takes a more familiar course and magmas erupt at the surface. In doing so, they must travel, either directly or in stages, through the crust. In the Andes, this can be thick or thin (Figure 4.2d), old or young (Figure 4.2c) depending on location. The Andes thus provide another natural experiment—one where we can examine the influence of the crust on the behaviour of subduction zone magmas. We will look at the results of this 'experiment' in the next Section and decipher the magmatic processes at work in the Andean crust.

4.3 MAGMATISM IN THE ANDES

4.3.1 Andean volcanic rocks and volcanoes

The diversity of geological features along the Andean plate margin extends to the range of volcanic land-forms. In some places, an isolated lava dome is the only sign of magmatism. Elsewhere, giant calderas tens of kilometres across are to be found. Some of these structures are so large that they were only recognized as calderas by using pictures taken from satellites. Plate 3.4 in the CPB shows the most spectacular of these—it is the Cerro Galan caldera in NW Argentina (Figure 4.2a). This structure is 40 km long and 20 km wide and formed by the collapse of a magma chamber's roof during the eruption of more than 1 000 km^3 of calc-alkaline dacite some 2.2 Ma ago. The resultant ignimbrites cover 10 000 km^2 to depths of 15 to 40 m. Other Andean caldera volcanoes that erupt silicic magmas are typically found in the Central Volcanic Zone (CVZ) defined in Figure 4.2a and ITQ 4.3(a).

Andesitic composite volcanoes (Figure 4.3a) are found throughout the volcanic zones, and total well over 1 000 volcanoes, although only 150 or so can be considered potentially active. These erupt lavas and ash from vents on the summit and flanks of the cones. An example we shall come to shortly is Lascar (Figure 4.3b) in the CVZ (Figure 4.2a), which produces explosive ash eruptions every few years.

(a)   (b)

Figure 4.3 (a) The Paniri volcano, Chile, is a large andesite composite cone. It rises more than 2 000 m above the surroundings to a peak 6 000 m above sea-level. (b) Lascar volcano in northern Chile is currently active and comprises two overlapping andesite cones. The lobate front of a thick lava flow is seen left of centre.

Why should silicic calderas be most common in the CVZ rather than the other volcanic zones of the Andes? If basalt enters the crust in all of the volcanic zones, then why should dacite be more commonly erupted at the surface in only a certain part of the Andes?

The processes that occur in the crust must determine the ultimate nature of the erupted magmas, so to answer the above questions we need to look for clues in the crustal geology of the volcanic zones.

What is the difference between the crust in the CVZ and that of the other volcanic zones?

As you found from Figure 4.2a, c and d when answering ITQ 4.3, the CVZ is the only one to lie on thick Precambrian crust. Many of these Precambrian rocks are silicic gneisses, in contrast to more mafic Palaeozoic metasediments within the basement of the NVZ, SVZ and AVZ. So, it is tempting to suggest that silicic magmas abound in the CVZ because the silicic crust there becomes melted and incorporated into the magmas, whereas in other volcanic zones a more mafic crust has failed to modify the intruded magmas. If these chemical interactions between mantle-derived magmas and the crust actually occur, then we should be able to see definite evidence in the geochemistry of the lavas, and this is the target of the following Section.

4.3.2 Contamination of Andean magmas by South American crust: theory

How are we to recognize magmas that have been contaminated by crustal material?

Well, xenoliths of partly digested metamorphic or sedimentary rocks caught up in lavas give an obvious illustration of crustal contamination. But what if the crustal rocks have been completely disaggregated and assimilated into the magma? In this case, we have to rely on interpreting the chemical composition of the lava.

In Section 3.4, we developed ways of studying trace element data to recognize the operation of fractional crystallization. Starting with the Rayleigh fractionation equation, it was shown that a variation diagram drawn on log–log graph paper, in which any two trace elements are plotted against each other, will define a straight line if fractional crystallization has been operative. This criterion allowed us to recognize fractional crystallization as the prime controller of magma composition at Santorini. Also at Santorini, however, are magmas formed by mixing two different magmas that were related by a previous episode of fractional crystallization (e.g. Figures 3.30, 3.32). Although these mixed magmas did not plot on the Rayleigh fractionation trends (e.g. Figures 3.29, 3.30), they did not require contamination by foreign material to account for their chemical and mineralogical compositions. Thus, failure to plot on a straight line log–log trend does not immediately imply a role for crustal contamination. In order to make crustal contamination a necessary component of a magma series' evolutionary history, it is necessary to show that fractional crystallization *and* mixing cannot account for all the chemical data. There is a special property of the Rayleigh fractionation equation that allows us to do this easily.

Consider two trace elements, A and B, with bulk partition coefficients D_A and D_B. The concentrations of A and B in a parental magma are C_{0A} and C_{0B}, and in a fractionated magma are C_A and C_B. From the Rayleigh fractionation equation

$$C_A = C_{0A}F^{D_A-1}$$

$$C_B = C_{0B}F^{D_B-1}$$

such that the ratio of these trace elements is

$$\frac{C_A}{C_B} = \frac{C_{0A}F^{D_A-1}}{C_{0B}F^{D_B-1}} = \frac{C_{0A}}{C_{0B}}F^{(D_A-1)-(D_B-1)} = \frac{C_{0A}}{C_{0B}}F^{D_A-D_B} \qquad (4.1)$$

The trace element ratio will change during fractionation (since it is a function of F) *unless $D_A = D_B$.* When the bulk partition coefficients are equal, we get the special result

$$\frac{C_A}{C_B} = \frac{C_{0A}}{C_{0B}} F^0 = \frac{C_{0A}}{C_{0B}} \tag{4.2}$$

i.e. the trace element ratio remains constant during fractional crystallization when $D_A = D_B$. In graphical terms, equation 4.2 means that a suite of lavas when plotted on a variation diagram of C_A versus C_B will define a straight line passing through the origin. Furthermore, mixing between two magmas that plot on this straight fractionation trend must yield a mixed magma with the same trace element ratio.

If we can identify two elements with identical bulk partition coefficients, then the ratio of these elements will remain constant in a magma series influenced only by fractional crystallization and magma mixing. Variable trace element ratios must indicate the additional operation of some contamination process by a contaminant that has a different trace element ratio from the parental magma.

To test out this theory on some real volcanic rocks, we need to choose two suitable trace elements. A compatible trace element (e.g. Sr, Ni, Cr, V) together with an incompatible trace element (e.g. Th, Rb, La, Ta, Zr, Y, Hf) certainly would not be appropriate, since, by their definitions, their bulk partition coefficients will be very different. Indeed, this feature causes a compatible versus incompatible trace element plot to be markedly curved, as we found in Figures 3.18a, 3.29 and 3.30.

> **ITQ 4.4** (a) Would you expect the bulk partition coefficients of two compatible trace elements to be identical (or nearly so)?
>
> (b) Would you expect the bulk partition coefficients of two incompatible trace elements to be identical (or nearly so)?

The low mineral K_D values for highly incompatible trace elements cause the bulk partition coefficient to be uniformly low, so the important conclusion is that *ratios of highly incompatible trace elements should remain constant during fractional crystallization (and mixing of these fractionated magmas) unless the magmas are contaminated by material having a different ratio of these incompatible trace elements.*

Before examining the incompatible trace element ratios in Andean magmas, an important extension to this discussion can be made. The reason why highly incompatible trace elements have such similar D values is because they have very similar chemical properties (brought about by distinctive ionic size and/or charge). The same argument can be made for different isotopes of the same trace element, particularly those of large atomic mass. So, even though Sr is a compatible trace element during the fractionation of feldspar-bearing magmas, the isotopes ^{87}Sr and ^{86}Sr, which you met in second level courses, will have essentially identical bulk partition coefficients. The isotopic ratio $^{87}Sr/^{86}Sr$ will not be affected by fractional crystallization (and mixing). This is why isotope geochemistry is so useful in keeping track of the processes involved in magma evolution.

So, we predict that both highly incompatible trace element ratios and isotopic ratios will remain constant in magma series unaffected by a compositionally distinct contaminant.

We can see that this is the case at Santorini. At that volcano, the two highly incompatible trace elements Rb and Th fall on a straight line passing through the origin (Figure 4.4a), and $^{87}Sr/^{86}Sr$ is essentially the same in all rock types (Figures 4.4b). Both of these plots indicate that contamination has not been a significant process at Santorini. This fits with our earlier findings (Sections 3.4.2, 3.4.3 and 3.5) that Santorini's magmas could be explained by fractional crystallization and magma mixing. The $^{87}Sr/^{86}Sr$ of Santorini's magmas is typical of the mantle source region of basalt.

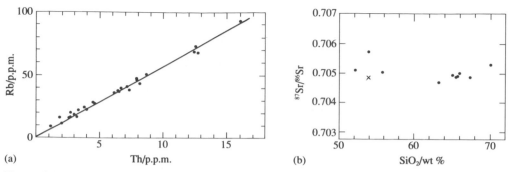

(a)   Th/p.p.m.   (b) SiO_2/wt %

Figure 4.4 (a) Plot of Rb against Th for Santorini lavas defines a straight line passing through the origin. The slope of this line gives a Rb/Th ratio of *c.* 5.7. (b) The isotope ratio $^{87}Sr/^{86}Sr$ of Santorini's lavas is virtually constant (*c.* 0.705) and shows no systematic variation with rock composition. (Points, fractionated magmas; cross, mixed magma)

4.3.3 Contamination of Andean magmas by South American crust: observation

Can we find evidence for crustal contamination of Andean magmas? We will look at just three volcanoes. Cerro Galan and Lascar (Figures 4.2a and 4.3b) are in the CVZ and rest on Precambrian basement where the crust is 35 to 50 km thick. Our third volcano, Puyehue, is an andesitic composite cone in the SVZ (Figure 4.2a). Here the crust is about 35 km thick and consists primarily of Mesozoic volcanic and sedimentary rocks on a Palaeozoic basement. These three volcanoes thus erupt magmas that are exposed to different thicknesses and types of crust during their evolution. Will this mean they will have suffered different amounts of crustal contamination? The initial strontium isotope ratios, $^{87}Sr/^{86}Sr$, of rocks from our three volcanoes are plotted against SiO_2 in Figure 4.5.

> **ITQ 4.5** Examine Figure 4.5 and comment on possible interpretations of the magmatic processes at Cerro Galan, Lascar and Puyehue.

The geochemical evidence suggests that the magmas beneath Lascar and Cerro Galan assimilate material with high $^{87}Sr/^{86}Sr$ as they evolve from basalt through to dacite. When you studied Sr isotopes in a second level course, you learnt that ancient continental crust can have some of the highest $^{87}Sr/^{86}Sr$ ratios known. This is because of the long times over which the parent isotope ^{87}Rb, which is relatively abundant in silicic continental rocks, decays to the daughter isotope ^{87}Sr. So, mantle-derived basalts that become contaminated by ancient silicic crust give rise to magmas with elevated $^{87}Sr/^{86}Sr$ ratios. This seems to be what we see at Lascar and Cerro Galan

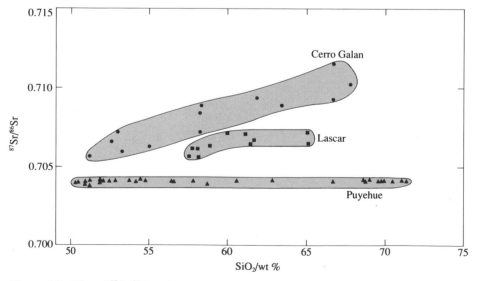

Figure 4.5 Plot of $^{87}Sr/^{86}Sr$ ratio against SiO_2 for rocks from Cerro Galan (circles), Lascar (squares) and Puyehue (triangles).

(Figure 4.5), and we can easily understand this since both of these CVZ volcanoes lie on Precambrian basement. (Strictly, we should talk about the rocks' initial isotope ratios, $(^{87}Sr/^{86}Sr)_0$, i.e. the ratio at the time when the rocks formed. In our Andean examples, however, the rocks are sufficiently young for the increase in $^{87}Sr/^{86}Sr$ due to decay of ^{87}Sr since the time of their eruption to be negligible.)

At Cerro Galan, there is also field evidence of crustal contamination. Plate 3.5a shows a xenolith of silicic gneiss collected from a basaltic andesite lava. In thin section (Plate 3.5b), the xenolith is seen to have been partially molten, with glass distributed between the quartz and feldspar crystals. The hot basaltic andesite has clearly been in the process of digesting the crustal xenolith and some of the feldspar is clouded, similar to the sieve textures produced when sodic plagioclase is heated in a calcic mafic magma during magma mixing (cf. Figure 3.33). The existence of coherent xenoliths argues against a magma-mixing origin for these textures in this case, however, and points to an advanced stage of assimilation of pre-existing rock. Within the basaltic andesite itself, a quartz xenocryst (Plate 3.5c) is surrounded by a corona of tiny orthopyroxene crystals formed by the reaction

$$SiO_2 \quad + \quad (Mg,Fe)O \quad \rightarrow \quad (Mg,Fe)\,SiO_3$$
$$\text{quartz} \quad \text{in basalt liquid} \quad \text{orthopyroxene}$$

The petrographic evidence clearly supports our geochemical argument for crustal contamination being an important process in the evolution of Cerro Galan's magmas.

At Puyehue, there is no evidence for contamination of the magma by rocks with an $^{87}Sr/^{86}Sr$ ratio that is different from that of the magmas (Figure 4.5). Of course, this is not to say that crustal contamination has not happened at all. Perhaps there was a contaminant that just happened to have the same $^{87}Sr/^{86}Sr$ as the magma.

> **ITQ 4.6** Apart from looking at a plot of $^{87}Sr/^{86}Sr$ against SiO_2, what other kind of geochemical test could we use to check if Puyehue's magmas have experienced crustal contamination?

Analyses of Puyehue's lavas displayed in Figure 4.6 clearly show a constant Rb/Th ratio, so it seems unlikely that crustal contamination has been significant at Puyehue. Its magmas are more likely to have evolved solely by fractional crystallization and magma-mixing processes.

So, although crustal contamination is not important in all arc volcanoes, there are some where pre-existing crust becomes mobilized by the incoming magmas. The end result is a crust that has both grown by addition of magma from the mantle and been 'reorganized' by the melting and assimilation of pre-existing crust into rising magmas.

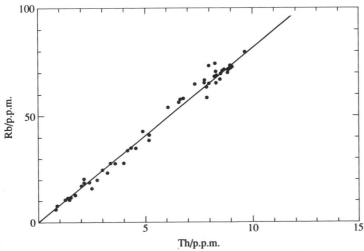

Figure 4.6 Plot of Rb against Th for Puyehue lavas. The data fall close to a straight line that passes through the origin. The slope of this line reveals that the Rb/Th ratio of this suite of lavas is approximately 8.1.

4.3.4 Mechanisms of crustal contamination of magmas

We have seen that geochemical evidence can tell us that crustal contamination has occurred but it does not tell us why or how it has happened. This Section presents some ideas on how hot magma can melt and digest cooler silicic crustal material in order to produce a contaminated magma. We shall also be making some predictions about how the composition of the magma will change as a result of these assimilation processes. It will then be possible to look back at the geochemical data and understand the compositional diversity of different volcanoes in terms of reworking of existing crust and the growth of crust from mantle-derived magmas. That is, we want to discover whether most of the igneous rocks in the Andes represent new crust or are just remobilized old crust.

An obvious constraint that will determine whether a magma can heat and melt crustal rocks is that the magma must be hotter than the melting temperature (solidus) of the crust. This means that high-temperature magmas—basalt at 1 200–1 250 °C or so—will be the most likely to assimilate parts of the crust. In addition, rocks such as granite with a solidus of 750 °C will require less heat energy to melt than will basic crust, which may only start to melt above 1 100 °C. The temperature of the crust prior to magma intrusion will also be important, as it will take more thermal energy to heat the upper crust from say 250 °C to 750 °C ($\Delta T = 500$ °C) than to heat hotter and deeper crust from 550 °C to 750 °C ($\Delta T = 200$ °C). The relative amounts of basalt and crust will also govern their final temperatures and so determine whether or not the crust can melt. There is more to the process of contamination than just having hot magma in contact with low-melting temperature crust. The way in which heat exchange occurs is important, and this is the starting point for looking at contamination.

Potentially, magma can become contaminated when it travels up through the crust in dykes and other conduits, and also as it sits and 'stews' in a magma chamber. The thermal and chemical contamination processes that occur in either case are quite different, however.

Contamination during flow in conduits

When magma flows through a conduit, it can move such that each particle of magma flows straight past its neighbours (Figure 4.7a). This is called **laminar flow**. Magma at the centre of the dyke advances most rapidly, while magma near the walls feels the resistive drag of viscosity and travels along more slowly. The magma at the walls remains in contact with the cold country rock and forms a chilled margin (Figure 4.7b), which seals the magma off from the country rock and prevents assimilation. For laminar flow, the magma passes through the crust uncontaminated.

If the magma's flow rate is sufficiently fast, the flow pattern becomes chaotic and turbulent. In **turbulent flow**, the magma moves in unpredictable eddies so that hot magma in the dyke's interior gets swirled up against the dyke walls and churned back into the dyke's interior, although the overall motion is still such that magma travels along the conduit (Figure 4.8a). As a consequence of the turbulence, hot magma is continuously exposed to the dyke walls and the country rock soon reaches a temperature close to that of the intruding magma. For a basalt at 1 200 °C, silicic country rock (with a liquidus of around 850 °C) will be rapidly melted and entrained into the flowing magma. The conduit walls become melted away (Figure 4.8b), widening the dyke, and this process is known as **thermal erosion**.

The efficiency of thermal erosion in producing contaminated magma can be summarized with reference to Figure 4.9, which shows that a critical aspect is the volumetric flow rate of hot magma through the conduit. For a low enough flow rate, there will be a laminar flow pattern causing heat transfer to be inefficient, chilled margins to form, and contamination to be prevented. For a given magma and dyke width, the transition from laminar flow to turbulent flow occurs over a narrow range of flow rates, so that the curve in Figure 4.9 jumps suddenly from zero contamination to significant contamination as the flow rate increases. Hot basalt magma has a low viscosity and can flow turbulently in dykes that are several metres

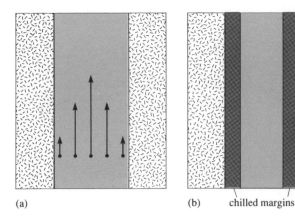

Figure 4.7 Cartoons of flow processes during laminar flow of magma in a dyke. (a) Individual particles of magma flow parallel with the dyke margins. Close to the edge of the dyke, magma is almost stationary, but in the centre, magma moves faster. The length of the arrows is proportional to the speed. (b) Slowly moving magma near the dyke walls loses heat rapidly to the country rock and solidifies as a chilled margin, protecting the fluid interior of the dyke from being contaminated.

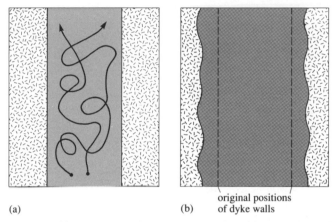

Figure 4.8 Cartoons of flow processes during turbulent flow of magma in a dyke. (a) Individual particles of magma flow along chaotic paths, although the net movement is upwards. (b) Because of the random motions in the magma (see (a)), hot magma from the centre of the dyke is continuously being brought into contact with the country rock. If the country rock melts at a temperature less than that of the basalt, then the walls of the dyke will fuse and become incorporated into the flowing magma. The dyke becomes widened by thermal erosion.

wide, leading to thermal erosion and contamination of the basalt. In even wider dykes, the flow rate will be higher, but because the magma travels through the dyke so rapidly it is exposed to the country rock for only a short time. The time available for assimilation is thus reduced as the flow rate increases, and the curve in Figure 4.9 turns downwards. The amount of contamination that a hot basalt magma can suffer during its passage through the crust thus depends heavily on the flow conditions involved. For a range of dyke widths, the degree of contamination will vary from zero to 10–20 per cent.

Whenever thermal erosion occurs, the contaminated magma will have a composition that plots on a mixing line between the original magma and the assimilated rock. This is a prediction that we can compare with the compositions of contaminated magmas such as those of Cerro Galan. We might be tempted to look for a straight line trend on a plot of ^{87}Sr (which has been enriched in ancient silicic crustal rocks) against Rb, say, to give us a large variation between the composition of primitive magma (low Rb, low radiogenic ^{87}Sr) and crustal contaminant (high Rb, high radiogenic ^{87}Sr). However, as you know, we can only measure the ratio $^{87}Sr/^{86}Sr$ in the rocks, so we have to plot $^{87}Sr/^{86}Sr$ against $Rb/^{86}Sr$, or, more conveniently, Rb/Sr. Indeed it is possible, but time consuming, to prove mathematically that *on a plot of $^{87}Sr/^{86}Sr$ against Rb/Sr, mixing is characterized by straight lines* and this is all that we need to know here.

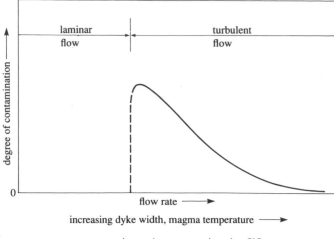

Figure 4.9 The amount by which a magma can be contaminated through thermal erosion depends on the parameters controlling the flow rate of magma in a dyke. Low flow rates come about in narrow dykes filled with relatively cool, silicic, viscous magma. In such cases, flow is laminar (Figure 4.7) and no contamination is possible. Hot, basic, low-viscosity magma in wide dykes flows at high rates in a turbulent fashion (Figure 4.8). This leads to thermal erosion of the country rock and contamination of the magma. At very high flow rates, the magma passes through the dyke so rapidly that it gets little chance to be contaminated, however. The maximum amount of contamination by thermal erosion occurs when the flow rate is just sufficient to cause turbulent flow.

ITQ 4.7 Figure 4.10 shows chemical data from Cerro Galan. Can the rock compositions be accounted for solely by varying degrees of assimilation of high $^{87}Sr/^{86}Sr$, high Rb/Sr crust into low $^{87}Sr/^{86}Sr$, low Rb/Sr basalt magma?

Thermal erosion does not seem to be an important process in the Andes, at least for the magmas that get erupted and analysed. There is always a possibility that the most primitive magmas do get contaminated by thermal erosion during their passage from the mantle into a crustal magma chamber. Subsequent processes in that chamber may then overprint any chemical signature of the previous contamination event. If we are really to get to grips with the contamination processes that account for the variable isotope ratios in Figures 4.5 and 4.10, we must consider how contamination is achieved in magma chambers.

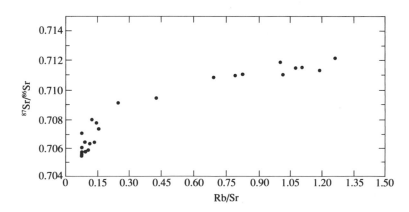

Figure 4.10 $^{87}Sr/^{86}Sr$ versus Rb/Sr plot of Cerro Galan volcanic rocks.

Contamination in magma chambers

The magma in a chamber loses heat to its surroundings. If there is insufficient heat to melt the enclosing country rock, then crystals will grow over the chamber walls; the magma will differentiate and cannot be contaminated. The alternative case, where the magma is capable of melting the country rock, is of interest here. In general, crustal melts will be more silicic than the basic magma responsible for their creation, and this will govern how any contamination process will operate. The reason lies with the density difference between acidic and basic magmas.

Are acidic magmas more or less dense than basic magmas?

Because they have low iron contents, acidic magmas such as rhyolite have lower densities than basic magmas, so melted crustal rocks are going to be less dense than basalts. To see why this has important implications for contamination processes, we need to consider which parts of the chamber's boundaries get melted. Two examples illustrate the major points–melting of the roof only and melting of the floor only.

The roof melting case can occur when a chamber of hot basalt is emplaced at the junction between rock layers with low and high melting temperatures (Figure 4.11). The less refractory, silicic, layer forms the chamber lid in this scenario. In the most extreme case of roof-melting, these roof rocks become completely molten, producing a silicic magma layer that remains floating on the hot convecting layer of basalt beneath. In slightly different circumstances, the roof rock may melt incompletely. If the partially melted region becomes disaggregated, the silicic liquid fraction will still float on the basalt, but blocks of unmelted roof rocks can fall through this layer into the hot basalt, which then becomes contaminated. The end-product is a layer of silicic magma formed by crustal melting above a basic magma that may have assimilated some foundered roof material or experienced some fractional crystallization as a result of losing heat to the roof (Figure 4.11).

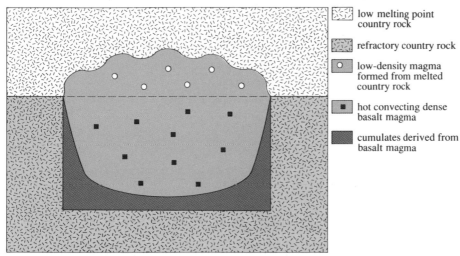

low melting point country rock

refractory country rock

low-density magma formed from melted country rock

hot convecting dense basalt magma

cumulates derived from basalt magma

Figure 4.11 Cartoon of a magma chamber containing basalt which is melting the overlying rocks. The melted rocks are silicic and so have a low density; they therefore float on top of the denser basalt. Meanwhile, crystals grow on the refractory (non-melting) margins of the chamber to build up a mass of cumulate rocks.

When it is the floor that melts, a totally different situation is created (Figure 4.12). The low density of the silicic melt formed on the chamber floor causes it to float off into the convecting interior of the chamber. Rather than staying as a separate magma, the crustal material gets mixed into the hot magma. This magma can also experience fractional crystallization if cumulate crystals grow and segregate on the stable (non-melting) boundaries of the chamber. A homogeneous magma is thus generated by simultaneous assimilation of the country rock and fractional crystallization of the contaminated magma. This rather involved process is known simply as the **AFC (assimilation with fractional crystallization)** process.

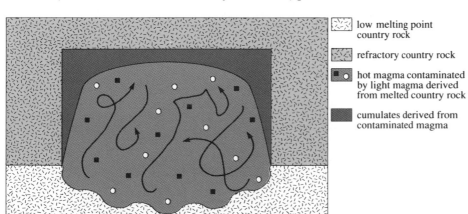

low melting point country rock

refractory country rock

hot magma contaminated by light magma derived from melted country rock

cumulates derived from contaminated magma

Figure 4.12 Cartoon of a magma chamber containing basalt which is melting the underlying rock. The liquid formed during melting is less dense than basalt, so it rises up into the convecting basalt and the two liquids become homogenized, resulting in a magma that has undergone crustal contamination. On the non-melting margins of the chamber, crystals grow from the contaminated magma to form cumulate rocks. The contaminated magma evolves by assimilation and fractional crystallization—i.e. AFC.

In some real magma chambers, the roof, floor and walls might melt, so there is great scope for complexity, particularly if we bear in mind that the chamber can receive inputs of fresh magma from below every so often. None the less, we have made sufficient progress to start considering the geochemical data again.

Magmas generated through an AFC process will, by definition, show compositional trends that combine those for assimilation and for fractional crystallization. We can predict what such a trend will look like by considering the AFC process as a series of steps alternating between assimilation and fractional crystallization. A graphical approach is taken, using a plot of $^{87}Sr/^{86}Sr$ versus Rb/Sr to understand the AFC process occurring during the interaction of a basalt (low $^{87}Sr/^{86}Sr$, low Rb/Sr) with continental crust having high $^{87}Sr/^{86}Sr$ and high Rb/Sr. To bring what you already know about the behaviour of $^{87}Sr/^{86}Sr$ and Rb/Sr during magmatic processes into focus, answer the following.

> **ITQ 4.8** (a) During contamination of basaltic magma by silicic crust, what will happen to (i) $^{87}Sr/^{86}Sr$ and (ii) Rb/Sr?
>
> (b) During fractional crystallization, what will happen to (i) $^{87}Sr/^{86}Sr$ and (ii) Rb/Sr?

During AFC, all of the effects you accounted for in answering ITQ 4.8 must occur. On a plot of $^{87}Sr/^{86}Sr$ against Rb/Sr (Figure 4.13), the first increment of crust to be assimilated by basalt (point a) will shift the magma's composition along the indicated mixing line to some point b. The length of the line ab reflects how much crust has been assimilated. Fractional crystallization of this magma will increase its Rb/Sr ratio by an amount that depends on the bulk distribution coefficients D_{Rb} and D_{Sr}, and the amount of crystallization. In the fractionation step of the AFC process, the magma evolves along a horizontal path to point c. A further increment of contamination moves the composition up along another mixing line, to point d, before fractional crystallization changes the composition to e. As the magma evolves, it becomes cooler, so the amount of assimilation decreases as the AFC process progresses. In addition, D_{Sr} increases as the magma becomes more silicic because the partition coefficient for Sr between plagioclase and liquid is larger in silicic magmas containing sodic plagioclase than in basic magmas with more calcic plagioclase. Sr thus becomes increasingly more depleted by fractional cystallization as the magma evolves. The effects of lower magma temperature and increasing D_{Sr} are to cause the contamination steps ab, cd, ef to become shorter and the fractionation steps bc,

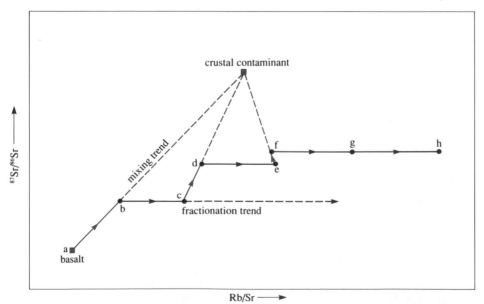

Figure 4.13 The chemical evolution of magma undergoing AFC (assimilation with fractional crystallization) can be seen on a plot of $^{87}Sr/^{86}Sr$ against Rb/Sr. Assimilation (red) produces magmas that lie on a straight line mixing trend between the magma and continental crust. Fractional crystallization (black) produces magmas with increased Rb/Sr but unchanged $^{87}Sr/^{86}Sr$. Alternating episodes of assimilation and fractional crystallization approximates the behaviour when both processes occur simultaneously. The sequence of magma formed by AFC (a,b,c,d,e,f,g and h) scatter around a curved trend.

de, fg to become longer. The magma can eventually lose its ability to melt its surroundings, and will evolve solely by fractional crystallization (f to g to h).

Unlike a straightforward mixing line, the AFC trend defined by a smooth path passing close to points a to h in Figure 4.13 is curved. Furthermore, unlike mixing, the AFC trend does not converge on the composition of the contaminant.

Hopefully, you will recognize the pattern shown by the Cerro Galan rocks (Figure 4.10) in the hypothetical trend of Figure 4.13. The simplest conclusion is that the Cerro Galan magmas were contaminated by crustal material during AFC processes occurring in a magma chamber. The large volume of the Cerro Galan ignimbrites (more than 1 000 km^3) and the presence of a large collapse caldera provide evidence of a substantial magma chamber—one of the basic requirements for AFC to be possible. Such huge volumes of dacitic magma would seem to require a considerable amount of crustal melts and the origin of these magmas may have involved an episode of roof melting.

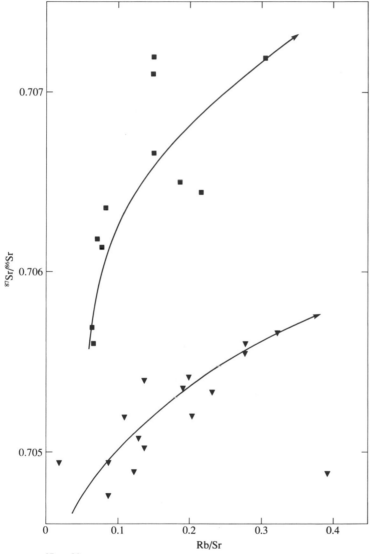

Figure 4.14 $^{87}Sr/^{86}Sr$ versus Rb/Sr plot for Lascar (squares) and Marmolejo (triangles) volcanic rocks.

For Lascar, an $^{87}Sr/^{86}Sr$ versus Rb/Sr plot (Figure 4.14) shows the curved trend typical of AFC, although the data are rather scattered, which could mean that the assimilated rocks had diverse compositions. Also shown on Figure 4.14 are data from the composite cone Marmolejo, which lies about 750 km north of Puyehue near the northern end of the SVZ.

> **ITQ 4.9** One andesite sample from Marmolejo plots separately from the others. Suggest how this sample could have achieved its 'unusual' composition.

Clearly, the degree to which crustal contamination influences Andean magmas is variable. At some volcanoes, contamination does not occur (or is at least undetectable), and this is the case at Puyehue for example. Elsewhere (Cerro Galan, Lascar and Marmolejo), we found that AFC processes had notably modified the magmas. Presumably, this variability reflects differences in the melting temperatures of the crustal rock types throughout the Andes. Contamination has most usually occurred at volcanoes in the CVZ, where the intruded crust is thick and contains Precambrian silicic gneisses that are readily melted. In the other volcanic zones, the younger, often thinner, crust rarely contaminates the magmas, and as a result fractional crystallization (and probably magma mixing) remain the only significant magmatic processes in those regions.

So, what implications do our findings have for understanding crustal growth at subduction zones? Obviously, it would be wrong to think that the total volume of erupted magma represents the total addition of material from the mantle wedge to the crust. In fact, there are two reasons why we cannot equate the volume of volcanic rocks to the volume of new crust. Can you think what these reasons are?

Firstly, we have just seen that certain magmas have incorporated significant amounts of pre-existing crust during their sub-surface evolution. Some of the more silicic contaminated magmas such as the voluminous dacitic ignimbrites from Cerro Galan may even represent partial melts of crustal rocks and contain little in the way of mantle-derived magma. Thus, at least some erupted arc magmas comprise a mixture of mantle-derived and crust-derived materials. In this respect, the volcanics can be an overestimate of the mantle's contribution to new crust.

The second reason why erupted magmas can give a false impression of the amount of crustal growth stems from the fact that they are only the *output* from subduction zone volcanoes. The volcanoes are underlain by intrusive rocks such as plutons. These comprise frozen magmas that failed to erupt and also the cumulates that are complementary to the evolved erupted magmas. Thus, if basalt enters the crust from the mantle wedge but fractionated andesite is extruded from the crust onto the surface, then a crystalline residue of fractionating minerals must be left in the crust. Thus, the volcanics may actually be an underestimate of the amount of material added to the crust. We must take all of the plutonic rocks into account when drawing up the budget of magmatic additions to the crust. In the next Section, we examine the geology of eroded arcs and assess the full contribution of arc magmatism to crustal growth.

Summary

1 While island arc volcanoes generally erupt basalts and basaltic andesites of tholeiitic, or low-K, affinity, active continental margins erupt calc-alkaline (medium- to high-K) magmas dominated by andesites.

2 Magmatic processes at an active continental margin are illustrated by the volcanic rocks of the Andes. Along the western edge of the South American Plate, arc magmatism is confined to areas above steeply dipping ($>25°$) subducted lithosphere. Where the dip is less, volcanism is absent, apparently because subducted seamount chains and aseismic ridges increase the buoyancy of the slab and curtail partial melting of the mantle wedge.

3 Magma that enters the crust may assimilate pre-existing crust and so evolve to compositions that depend on the composition and melting temperature of the intruded crust. Silicic crust has a low solidus temperature, and is the type of crust most readily assimilated by hot basalt. This may explain why the magmas at active continental margins are more evolved (silica-rich) than those of oceanic island arcs.

4 Crustal contamination can alter the isotope ratios and ratios of highly incompatible trace elements of a magma. Fractional crystallization does not change these ratios.

5 Basalt formed by partial melting of the mantle has low $^{87}Sr/^{86}Sr$ in comparison to that of ancient silicic crust. Magmas that have been contaminated by ancient silicic crust will, therefore, have elevated $^{87}Sr/^{86}Sr$ ratios.

6 Crustal contamination can theoretically occur in two environments:
(i) Contamination caused by thermal erosion of conduit walls occurs only for high rates of turbulent magma flow and affects only the hottest, most primitive, basaltic

magmas. Mixing of basalt and the crustal contaminant yields a magma with a composition that plots on a linear mixing trend on an $^{87}Sr/^{86}Sr$ versus Rb/Sr plot.

(ii) In certain magma chambers, the roof can melt to produce a compositionally zoned chamber (Figure 4.11) in which silicic crustal melts are underlain by hot basic magma. In other cases, the melted country rocks are continuously blended into the fractionating magma chamber (Figure 4.12). This process is called assimilation with fractional crystallization, or AFC for short. The compositions of magmas resulting from AFC plot as a curved trend on an $^{87}Sr/^{86}Sr$ versus Rb/Sr diagram. The AFC trend does not converge on the composition of the crustal rocks that have contaminated the magmas, unlike a simple mixing trend.

7   In the Andes, the most obvious AFC trends are found at Central Volcanic Zone (CVZ) volcanoes such as Cerro Galan and Lascar. This is consistent with the occurrence of xenoliths of Precambrian silicic gneiss in certain basic lavas at Cerro Galan. In the CVZ, the crust of the active continental margin is being reworked and added to by hot basalt magmas that originated in the mantle wedge.

SAQS for SECTION 4

SAQ 4.1   Explain whether each of the following statements is true or false:

(a) The Andean crust is never more than 40 km thick.

(b) Subducting slabs have shallow dips and volcanoes are absent in regions where seamount chains have entered subduction zones.

(c) Thermal erosion of dyke walls is favoured when the magma flow pattern is turbulent.

(d) Crustal contamination is insignificant at all Andean volcanoes.

SAQ 4.2   Compare and contrast oceanic island arcs with active continental margins in terms of

(a) the compositional spread (SiO_2 range) of magmas.

(b) tholeiitic versus calc-alkaline nature of magma series.

(c) volcanic landforms.

SAQ 4.3   Why is ancient silicic crust more easily recognized as a crustal contaminant in magmas than is young basic crust, using Sr isotopes?

SAQ 4.4   Examine Figure 4.15, which shows the $^{87}Sr/^{86}Sr$ and Rb/Sr ratios of young rocks from two magma series from separate volcanoes. Give a reasoned interpretation of each magma series' evolution, and suggest to which section(s) of the Andean plate margin each volcano may belong. What other evidence could be used to strengthen your conclusions regarding magmatic processes?

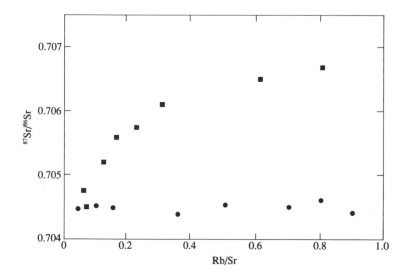

Figure 4.15   Plot of $^{87}Sr/^{86}Sr$ ratio against Rb/Sr for rocks in two volcanic magma series (series 1, circles; series 2, squares). For use with SAQ 4.4.

5 GEOLOGY OF ERODED ARCS: INSIGHTS ON THE GROWTH OF CONTINENTAL CRUST

Our studies of magmatic processes in Sections 3 and 4 have given an insight into the ways that magmas are modified during their intrusion into the crust and their transit through the crust. In this Section, we take the opposite approach and consider the modifications to the crust that have resulted from magmatism at subduction zones. This requires us to concentrate on the geology of arcs where the surface coating of volcanic rocks has been eroded away, allowing us access to the deeper manifestations of subduction zone processes on crustal geology.

There are four parts to Section 5. First, the petrology and geochemistry of plutonic arc rocks are introduced. Then, the subduction-related growth of two regions of Andean crust is examined. In the first example, growth was accomplished by igneous intrusion, and in the second example by a combination of intrusion and accretion of terranes of oceanic crust. The fourth part of this Section uses our knowledge of subduction zone geology to comment on the mechanisms and rates of crustal growth throughout Earth history.

5.1 PLUTONIC ROCKS IN ARCS

Active arcs are characterized by a chain of volcanoes spaced at 25 to 100 km intervals. As each volcano is underlain by a magma chamber, an eroded arc presents itself as a narrow belt of solidified plutons. In some cases, the number of plutons may be so great that an amalgamated body of plutons known as a **batholith** is formed. Linear batholiths, up to thousands of kilometres long and composed of hundreds or thousands of plutons, are found in the western Americas and are the legacy of Mesozoic and Tertiary subduction of the Pacific (e.g. Figure 5.1). These plutonic rocks range from gabbro to diorite to granite, being the intrusive equivalents of volcanic basalt, andesite and rhyolite.

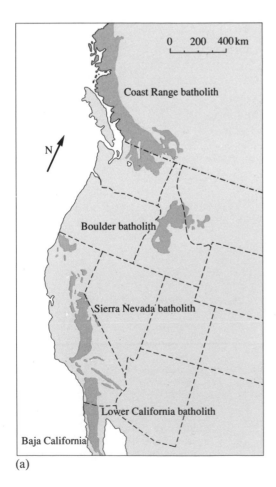

(a)

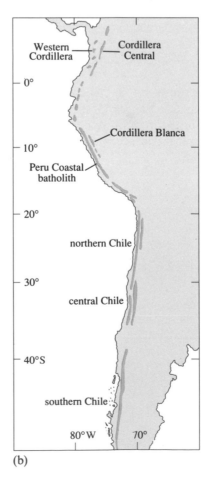

(b)

Figure 5.1 (a) The geology of western North America is dominated by four large batholiths (solid red) mostly emplaced during Mesozoic (mid-Cretaceous) time in response to the eastward subduction of Pacific ocean floor. (b) Mesozoic to Cenozoic batholiths (solid red) in South America.

The rigorous description of plutonic rocks relies heavily on their mineralogy. Being medium- to coarse-grained, a classification scheme based on modal mineralogy is simplest to apply. For example, gabbros contain mostly plagioclase and pyroxene, often with some olivine, and in some cases a little quartz and alkali feldspar that have crystallized from the last drop of highly evolved interstitial liquid. Diorite and granite will also be familar from second level studies. They contain quartz, alkali feldspar and plagioclase, together with hornblende and/or biotite and/or pyroxene, but the proportions of these minerals distinguish diorite (with less quartz and more mafic minerals) from granite. Since these, and transitional rock types, contain quartz, alkali feldspar and plagioclase, they can conveniently be considered as one group—the **granitoids**. An internationally used classification scheme for granitoids is based on the relative proportions of modal quartz, alkali feldspar and plagioclase as displayed on a ternary diagram—the **QAP (quartz–alkali feldspar–plagioclase) triangular diagram** (Figure 5.2). Different rock types have different quartz/feldspar and plagioclase/alkali feldspar ratios.

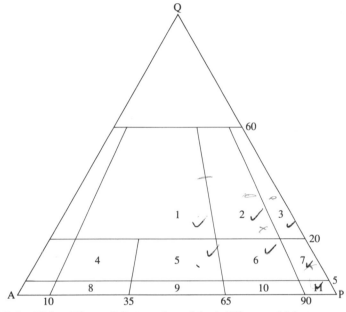

Figure 5.2 The modal Q (quartz)–A (alkali feldspar)–P (plagioclase) classification of granitoids. The numbered fields are as follows: 1, granite, 2, granodiorite; 3, tonalite; 4, quartz syenite; 5, quartz monzonite; 6, quartz monzodiorite; 7, quartz diorite; 8, syenite; 9, monzonite; 10, monzo-diorite; 11, gabbro and diorite.

ITQ 5.1   Using Figure 5.2 state the critical difference(s) between

(a) quartz monzonite and granite;

(b) tonalite and granodiorite;

(c) granodiorite and granite;

(d) quartz diorite and granodiorite;

(e) gabbro and quartz diorite.

In arcs, granites have the most evolved compositions and plot in the middle of the QAP triangle because they have relatively high quartz and alkali feldspar contents reflecting high SiO_2 and K_2O contents. Similarly, the less evolved magmas are represented by gabbro and diorite, which plot close to the P corner. Syenites and quartz syenites (fields 8 and 4) are formed from alkali-rich magmas, usually in a within-plate setting, and do not concern us further. In general, subduction zone plutonics fall in the fields numbered 1, 2, 3, 5, 6, 7 and 11 in Figure 5.2.

Plutonic rocks from subduction zones can also be compared chemically with those from other tectonic environments. In Block 2, you found that the normative mineralogy of a rock can be used for the purposes of classification. One scheme relies on the relative proportions of alkalis, calcium and alumina in the rock. If alumina is very abundant, then normative corundum (C: Al_2O_3) will be present and the rock is then termed peraluminous. If the alkalis are dominant, then normative acmite (Ac: $NaFeSi_2O_6$) is present. Between these extremes are the metaluminous rocks, and these have normative anorthite (An: $CaAl_2Si_2O_8$). As a rule, this threefold division correlates with tectonic settings, as given in Table 5.1. The differences arise from the different P–T conditions and compositions of the magmas' source regions, and in general subduction zone magmas are metaluminous.

Table 5.1 Designation of igneous rock types according to characteristic normative minerals, together with their typical tectonic settings

Tectonic setting	Characteristic normative mineral	Name
rift zone	acmite	peralkaline
subduction zone	anorthite	metaluminous
continental collision zones	corundum	peraluminous

On a much more local scale, plutons rarely consist of just one rock type. Many show a crudely concentric compositional variation, or zonation, typically with gabbro or diorite discontinuously exposed around their margins and granodiorite or granite at their centres. This pattern is due to inward solidification of a fractionating magma chamber and intrusion of more evolved magmas into the core of the pluton. The compositional variation in plutons is thus due to the same processes that we recognized in erupted magmas.

For discussing compositional differences between plutons from separate arcs, the tholeiitic/calc-alkaline division that we used in Section 3.3.1 (Figure 3.9 and 3.10) is of most use. Figures 5.3 and 5.4 illustrate the mineralogical and chemical compositions of two plutons. They are the Finger Bay pluton in the Aleutian island arc and the Senal Blanca complex in the continental margin of Peru.

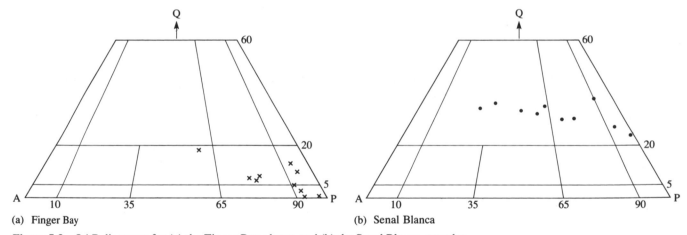

(a) Finger Bay

(b) Senal Blanca

Figure 5.3 QAP diagrams for (a) the Finger Bay pluton and (b) the Senal Blanca complex.

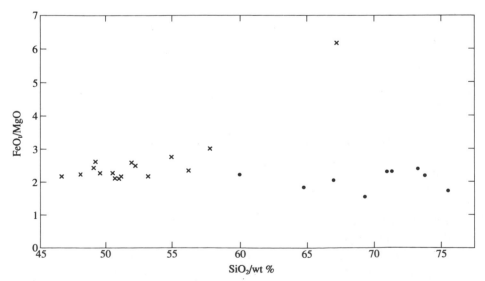

Figure 5.4 Plot of FeO_t/MgO against SiO_2 for rocks from the Finger Bay pluton (crosses) and the Senal Blanca complex (points).

ITQ 5.2 Compare and contrast the compositions of the island arc and continental margin plutons whose compositions are plotted in Figures 5.3 and 5.4 in terms of

(a) the range of SiO_2 contents;

(b) their tholeiitic or calc-alkaline composition;

(c) the mineralogy and range of rock types.

The plutons studied in ITQ 5.2 are rather extreme examples of subduction zone rocks, and a whole range of other plutons have features that lie between those of Finger Bay and Senal Blanca. None the less, these plutons bear out our findings from volcanic rocks. That is, arc magmas on oceanic crust (island arcs) tend to be mafic to intermediate tholeiitic magmas–they are gabbros, diorites and quartz monzonites. At continental margins, the magmas are intermediate to silicic, calc-alkaline and include granodiorite and granite, having relatively high quartz/feldspar ratios.

Another generalized difference is that continental margin plutons often reach considerable size (10 km across) and number, to constitute large batholiths parallel to the plate margin. In contrast, island arc plutons tend to be smaller and less numerous, forming a scattered chain of plutons.

We now have an outline of the building blocks of the plutonic belts that are related to subduction.

5.2 CRUSTAL GROWTH: THE PERUVIAN AND CHILEAN BATHOLITHS

Earlier in this Block, the natural laboratory of Andean volcanism provided several insights into the ways subduction-related magmas interact with the crust. In this and the next Sections, Andean batholiths (Figure 5.1b) provide other views of how subduction processes have formed, over many millions of years, a substantial volume of the Andean mountain belt (or orogenic zone). Evidence of subduction beneath western parts of South America dates back to the Palaeozoic, but the present configuration of the destructive margin became established in the Mesozoic. Since that time, the Andes have grown more-or-less continuously. The mechanisms of crustal growth south of Ecuador appear to have been constant for over 7 500 km length of plate margin. Here, crustal growth was associated with the emplacement of the Peruvian Coastal Batholith and the batholiths of the Cordillera Blanca and Chile (Figure 5.1b). Further north, in western Colombia, a different tectonic situation arose, and that is the subject of Section 5.3.

The most thoroughly studied Andean batholith is the Coastal Batholith of Peru (Figure 5.1b). It is 1 600 km long and 65 km wide, comprising about 1 000 plutons intruded at shallow depths (3–8 km) between 100 and 30 million years ago. This enormous structure has an estimated volume of 1 million cubic kilometres. The concerted study of the batholith and its surrounding rocks has involved many geologists, primarily from Britain and Peru, under the leadership of Professor W. S. Pitcher of the University of Liverpool and Dr E. J. Cobbing of the British Geological Survey. Their work underpins much of our understanding of Andean batholiths, and most geologists recognize the following picture over the 7 500 km from southern Ecuador to southern Chile.

During the Permo-Triassic, basic igneous rocks intruded an extensional basin on the continental margin, parallel with the present continental margin. During this early phase of the growth of the Andes, the continental crust was being thinned, split apart and transected by basaltic magmas.

In the mid-Cretaceous, compressive tectonics became established and brought about an important change in the way magmas interacted with the crust. During the period of extension, magmas could readily rise to the surface and erupt along fault-controlled fissures, but in the compressive regime their upward passage would have been closed off. Gabbroic intrusions formed and led to melting of the mafic crust and to fractional crystallization to produce granitoid magmas. These low-density magmas further stabilized the crust, leading to uplift and a true Andean mountain range started to grow. At the same time, the deep fault zones initiated during early Mesozoic extension channelled magmas into the crust. In this way, granitoid plutons were continuously emplaced into a narrow belt of flawed crust, establishing a batholith. Each increment of crustal growth stems from the arrival of basaltic magma, which then generated silicic magmas by fractional crystallization and/or crustal melting. This sequence is clearly seen in the concentric zoning of individual plutons from basic margins to silicic cores and in cross-cutting field relationships where granite or granodiorite intrudes already-solidified tonalite hosts. A two-stage sequence of compositional evolution thus occurs on the scale of a pluton several kilometres across and over its solidification time of no more than a million years. At the scale of the entire Andean belt—thousands of kilometres over 200 million years— a two-stage origin for Andean crustal growth is also apparent from our description of the region's history since the Mesozoic. Firstly, basic magma and thinned continental crust were formed during extension above an early Mesozoic subduction zone. Secondly, after this regime switched to being compressive, the new tectonic forces prevented subduction zone magmas rising directly to the surface. Instead, the magmas intruded and melted the young mafic crust to yield granitoids. Over time, individual plutons became amalgamated into huge batholiths, which have since been exposed by erosion of the mountainous Andes.

5.3 CRUSTAL GROWTH: COLOMBIAN ANDES

The geology of the Colombian Andes shows evidence for a style of crustal growth that is very different from that just described in Section 5.2. This part of the South American crust has grown by the accretion of displaced terranes, a concept that you met in Block 1A, Section 3.3. This Section shows you the evidence for this style of crustal growth.

5.3.1 Geology of western Colombia

The geological framework of western Colombia is closely linked to the four mountain belts (cordillera) running parallel with the coast (Figure 5.5). The Eastern Cordillera are a complex range of Precambrian and Palaeozoic igneous and metamorphic rocks overlain by sediment. They form the very northwestern edge of the South American craton.

The Central Cordillera is the highest mountain range (up to 5 800 m). Although areas of Precambrian basement are present here, the rocks are essentially a pre-Mesozoic metamorphic belt intruded by Mesozoic high-level calc-alkaline quartz monzonite, granodiorite and granite batholiths. The western edge of the Central Cordillera is defined by the Romeral Fault Zone, which separates the mountains from the Cauca–Patia Graben (Figure 5.5). The Graben contains Jurassic to early Cretaceous ocean floor basalt and gabbro intruded by granitoid plutons and with a cover of terrigenous sediments. Approximately 50 to 60 km west of the Romeral Fault Zone lies the Cauca–Patia Fault Zone, defining the eastern margin of the Western Cordillera. This range is composed of Upper Cretaceous ocean-floor basalts with intercalated marine sediments, and is intruded by Tertiary calc-alkaline plutons. The Coastal Cordillera in NW Colombia runs north along the coast into Panama and is made of altered Upper Cretaceous to Eocene ocean-floor basalt overlain by Tertiary sediments. All of the fault-bounded depressions between the Cordilleras contain thick deposits of Tertiary sediment—marine types in the Pacific Coastal Plain, terrigenous types inland.

The final geological feature of note is of course the active volcanic arc (the NVZ of the Andes introduced in Section 4.2) related to easterly subduction of the Nazca Plate. Most of the arc lies on the Central Cordillera, but it transgresses the Romeral Fault Zone in the south of the country (Figure 5.5). Andesitic calc-alkaline volcanism has been occurring here since the late Miocene. Western Colombia thus comprises a number of fault-bounded blocks of diverse basement rocks, variously intruded by plutons and/or covered by young sediments. Some patterns are present, however, and these will help you to piece together the geological evolution of this part of crust.

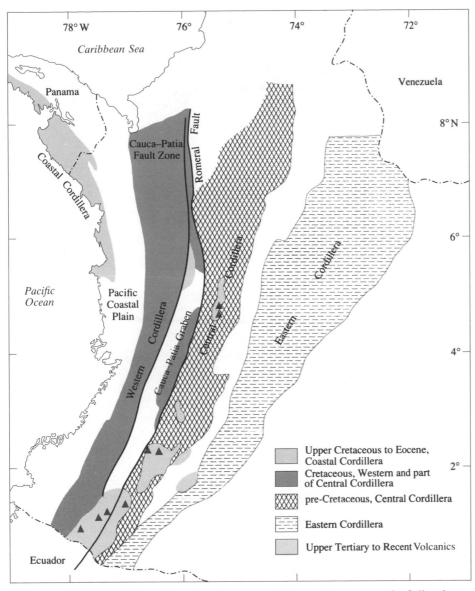

Figure 5.5 Geological sketch map of Colombia.

ITQ 5.3 From the above description and Figure 5.5, answer the following:

(a) Does the geology change across an east–west or north–south transect?

(b) On an east to west traverse, do the oldest rocks become generally younger or older?

(c) On this traverse, what changes occur in the nature of the basement rocks?

(d) Again on this traverse, do the ages of plutonic rocks change, and if so do they become younger or older in more westerly locations?

5.3.2 Crustal growth by the accretion of displaced terranes

The most obvious aspect of western Colombian geology is the change from pre-Mesozoic crystalline basement east of the Romeral Fault Zone to younger ocean-floor lithologies west of the Fault Zone. The striking contrast in crustal type and age is prime evidence for proposing the ocean crust in the Cauca–Patia Graben to be a displaced terrane accreted to South America by movement along the Romeral Fault Zone. The Upper Jurassic and Lower Cretaceous ocean crust has been named the Amaime Terrane, and the processes attending its emplacement, or docking, can be uncovered by studying the ages and geographical distribution of the granitoid intrusions. For instance, the fault movement must post-date the youngest basement which it cuts, but pre-date the oldest intrusions which cut across the fault.

The distribution of plutonic activity in time and space is seen from the geological map in Figure 5.6, which has been simplified to highlight the Romeral and Cauca–Patia Fault Zones. Radiometric dating of the intrusions has revealed that magmatic activity occurred in five pulses, labelled episodes A to E.

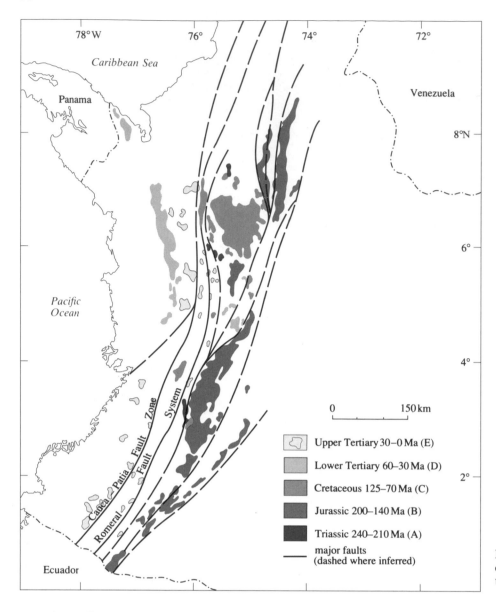

Figure 5.6 Map showing the outcrops of plutons within Colombia and the major fault systems.

According to Figure 5.6, where are the Triassic and Jurassic plutons located?

They are all east of the Romeral Fault Zone, within the Central Cordillera. The large area of these batholiths, and the fact that these are rather silicic granitoids, are characteristic of their association with old crystalline continental basement.

> **ITQ 5.4** Looking carefully at Figure 5.6, identify the ages of plutons that cut the Romeral Fault Zone.

The answer to ITQ 5.4 implies that the Romeral Fault Zone was active before the Cretaceous. In fact, the oldest pluton cutting the fault, has an age of 124 ± 6 Ma—in the Lower Cretaceous. The Amaime terrane must have docked with South America close to the Jurassic/Cretaceous time boundary. Best estimates for the docking age are 125–130 Ma. Episode E plutonism then occurred after the Amaime terrane had become part of South America.

How does the more westerly geology of Colombia, beyond the Cauca–Patia Fault Zone, relate to the Amaime terrane? Immediately west of the fault, the rocks of the Western Cordillera are Upper Cretaceous ocean floor. They are thus younger than the Amaime terrane, and have been suggested to be another displaced terrane that must have docked with South America along the Cauca–Patia Fault Zone sometime after 125 Ma.

In terms of dating the docking of the Western Cordillera, it turns out that in this case the plutonic geology is not very helpful, and some other method is needed.

Distinctive lithologies in the Western Cordillera terrane will provide a unique component to any locally derived sediment. Only those sediments in the Cauca–Patia Graben that were deposited after the docking and uplift of the Western Cordillera will contain the distinctive lithologies. It turns out that dolerite and chert clasts, which could only have been derived from the Upper Cretaceous rocks of the Western Cordillera, are present in the deformed lowermost succession of Palaeocene to Eocene sediments outcropping along the western margin of the Cauca–Patia Graben. Clearly, these sediments accumulated while the Cauca–Patia Fault Zone was still causing deformation, but after the Western Cordillera was more or less in its present position. This indicates a docking time in the lower Palaeocene—about 60 million years ago.

These two examples of terrane accretion show that the process of crustal growth in western Colombia has been very different from that elsewhere in the Andes.

5.3.3 Mechanisms of terrane accretion

While it may be satisfying to see the geology of an area such as Colombia in terms of terrane accretion, this leads to the question of why this part of the crust evolved by a combination of subduction-related calc-alkaline magmatism and accretionary tectonics along strike–slip faults. There would appear to be a paradox in a destructive plate margin allowing accretion processes. The natural place to start resolving this paradox is by looking at the evolution in time and space of subduction and accretion. Recall that the accretion of the Amaime terrane and the Western Cordillera took place at c. 125–130 Ma and c. 60 Ma respectively.

> Of the five magmatic episodes identified on Figure 5.6, which ones coincide with the accretion events?

Although the very beginnings of episodes C and D may have coincided with the accretion events, it is uncertain whether they truly overlap. It is mechanically more likely that accretion took place during lulls in magmatism. During magmatic episodes, oceanic lithosphere approaches the continental crust head-on, or at a high angle, and consequently subducts, triggering the familiar chain of events leading to arc magmatism. During accretion, the oceanic lithosphere passes the continent obliquely such that slivers of ocean crust become sheared off along strike–slip faults onto the continental margin. Under these conditions, subduction does not take place, and no calc-alkaline magmas can form. A survey of currently active volcanic arcs suggests that the downgoing plate must approach at more than 25 ° to the plate boundary for magmatism to occur.

Given the above constraints on the influence of ocean–continent convergence angles on tectonic and magmatic processes, it is possible to propose a series of events that can explain the observed geology of Colombia. One model, which accounts for some of the most obvious events before, during and after the accretion of the Western Cordillera, has been proposed by the British Geological Survey scientists working in Colombia, and is illustrated in greatly simplified form in Figures 5.7. This model also incorporates the evolution of the Coastal Batholith of Peru, so it encompasses a large part of the Andes and inevitably some details have been sacrificed for the sake of simplicity.

Figure 5.7a shows the plate margin 90 million years ago, with subduction from the southwest generating batholiths in the Central Cordillera of Colombia (episode C in Figure 5.6) and the Coastal Batholith of Peru. This is a consequence of the high convergence angles all along the plate margin. The geological record shows plutonism to have been sparse in Ecuador, and this may signify the subduction of buoyant seamounts (cf. Section 4.2) or some sort of offset in the trench related to transcurrent faulting, but we have ignored these conjectured complexities here.

At 60 Ma (Figure 5.7b), the oceanic plate approached from the SSW and subducted beneath Peru, sustaining additions to the Coastal Batholith. The convergence angle in the Colombian region is very small, however, forcing a sliver of ocean floor to be accreted onto the plate edge by movement along the Cauca–Patia Fault Zone. This

76

is the ocean crust that develops into the Western Cordillera. Because of the oblique convergence and terrane accretion, subduction beneath Colombia ceases, preventing the generation of magmas.

At 40 Ma (Figure 5.7c), easterly subduction has revived magmatism (episode D) in Colombia and continues to produce magmas for the Coastal Batholith.

It may seem offhand to propose these switches in plate motion, but there is a precedent in that hot-spot traces show abrupt inflections caused by equally abrupt changes in sea-floor spreading directions. The best-known example is the bend in the Hawaii–Emperor seamount chain in the NW Pacific (TMOE and Block 1A, Figure 3.2a) that was established about 40 Ma ago, when northward motion of the plate changed to northwestward motion. Similar effects have been observed in hot-spot tracks in the SE Pacific and give a sound basis for the switching subduction directions invoked in Figures 5.7a to 5.7c. Extrapolation to older times is tricky, however, but a similar set of events were probably associated with the Early Cretaceous accretion of the Amaime terrane during the interval between plutonic episodes B and C.

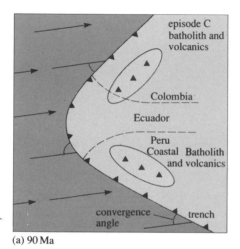
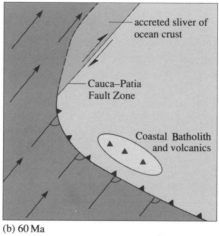
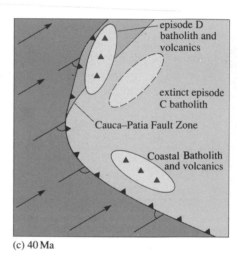

(a) 90 Ma   (b) 60 Ma   (c) 40 Ma

Figure 5.7 Cartoons showing the effects of different convergence angles between the Nazca Plate and NW South America on the geological history of Colombia and Peru. See text for details. The configuration (a) 90 Ma ago, (b) 60 Ma, (c) 40 Ma.

The important point is that the geometry of the plate margin and the direction of convergence influence the response of the crust. When these conspire to give a high angle of convergence, then subduction occurs, and this produces magmatic inputs to the crust. For oblique convergence, subduction does not occur, and terrane accretion is favoured.

5.4 THE RATE OF CRUSTAL GROWTH AT SUBDUCTION ZONES

In studying the last two Sections, you will have become increasingly aware that considerable parts of the continental crust owe their existence to subduction processes. The continental crust is actually growing in volume. Where is the new material coming from?

Subduction zone magmas and accreted ocean crust are ultimately derived from the upper mantle. So crustal growth occurs at the expense of the mantle, but how rapidly does this take place? Can you think how you could start to get an answer to this question? If we can estimate the volume added to the crust over a known time, then these two figures can give us the crustal growth rate.

> **ITQ 5.5** The entire volume of the Coastal Batholith of Peru was intruded over many millions of years; the details were given in Section 5.2. Use those details to estimate the crustal growth rate in this part of South America.

What does your answer to ITQ 5.5 actually represent? You have taken the *estimated* volume of intruded magma to be the total volume of material added to the crust. There are two problems associated with this, however. First of all, it is difficult to account accurately for the unexposed roots of the batholith and the eroded roof zones and volcanics. Secondly, even if the volumes of these igneous rocks were known precisely, this would overestimate the volume of material added to the crust because, as we saw in Section 4.3.3, certain magmas have been formed by melting and digestion of pre-existing crustal rocks. The intrusion rate of magma into the upper crust will give an inaccurate measure of the growth rate of the whole arc crust. If we are to account for all of the material added to the crust, we need a different approach—one that relies on the ability of geophysical methods to see into the deep crust.

Do you recall how the geophysical picture of arc crust differs from that of 'normal' crust?

In Section 4.1 (see Figure 4.1), we found that the crust in magmatic arcs is thicker than in adjacent non-arc regions. In particular, the lower crust is often thickened as a result of subduction processes. A cross-section through the active continental margin in the central Andes is given in Figure 5.8. A deep keel, shallow intrusive rocks and surface volcanics have been added to the crust, resulting in considerable thickening. The excess cross-sectional area multiplied by the length of the arc is then equal to the added crustal volume. Dividing this by the age of subduction-related magmatism gives the crustal growth rate. For every kilometre of arc in the central Andes, about thirty cubic kilometres must get added to the crust every million years in order to account for the cross-section in Figure 5.8. Similar rates have been measured by the same method at other active continental margins and also in island arcs. The average growth rate is 30 km^3 Ma^{-1} per kilometre of arc, i.e. 30 km^3 Ma^{-1} km^{-1}.

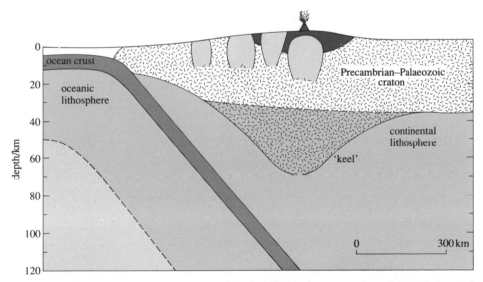

Figure 5.8 Schematic east–west cross section showing an interpretation of the structure of the South American Plate margin in the central Andes.

ITQ 5.6 Using your answer to ITQ 5.5, calculate the growth rate of the Peruvian Coastal Batholith in terms of the volume rate per kilometre of batholith length.

You should have found that the Peruvian Batholith grew at about a third of the rate estimated for the entire arc crust. The emplacement of plutons in the upper crust must, therefore, have been accompanied by intrusion into lower parts of the crust which we only see by using geophysical techniques (Figures 4.1 and 5.8).

ITQ 5.7 (a) The total length of magmatic arcs on the Earth is 37 000 km. What is the current total rate of crustal growth at subduction zones?

(b) The volume of the continental crust is $7.8 \times 10^9 \, \text{km}^3$, while the age of the Earth is 4.55×10^9 years. What is the average rate of continental growth?

Has the rate of continental growth increased, decreased or stayed roughly constant throughout Earth history?

The average long-term rate of crustal growth is considerably faster than that which has been measured at subduction zones. If the current rate had operated for 4.55 billion years, then the volume of continental crust should be $1.1 \times 4.5 \times 10^9 = 5 \times 10^9 \, \text{km}^3$. This is only about two thirds of the observed volume. To account for the extra 2.8 billion cubic kilometres of crust, the growth rate of the continents must have been significantly faster during earlier periods of Earth history. This might have been because plate tectonic movements were more vigorous or some other more productive process was responsible for crustal growth. Working out the geological processes occurring during early Earth history is beyond the scope of this Block, which seeks to understand geologically recent arc processes. The nature of early crustal growth, as seen in the geology of ancient crust, will be exposed in Block 5.

Summary

1 Plutonic rocks containing modal quartz, plagioclase and alkali feldspar are called granitoids. They are classified on the basis of their quartz/feldspar and plagioclase/alkali feldspar ratios. Granitoid classification (granite, granodiorite, tonalite, monzonite, etc.) is thus based on the QAP triangular diagram (Figure 5.2).

2 Granitoids in arc settings are typically metaluminous (normative anorthite), in contrast with those from continental rifts (peralkaline: normative acmite) and continental collision zones (peraluminous: normative corundum).

3 The roots of arc volcanoes are exposed in eroded arcs, and form plutonic belts and batholiths that lie parallel to the ancient convergent plate margin.

4 Arc plutonics formed in continental crust are generally calc-alkaline and include the more silicic granitoids such as granite and granodiorite. In eroded oceanic island arcs, granitoids are more usually tholeiitic, and less silicic rock types (gabbros, diorite, quartz diorite, quartz monzodiorite) are dominant. These chemical patterns are similar to those found in volcanic suites from active continental margins and oceanic island arcs.

5 Individual plutons are often compositionally zoned, becoming more silicic towards their centres.

6 In the Andes south of Ecuador, large calc-alkaline batholiths (e.g. the Coastal Batholith of Peru) have been emplaced since mid-Jurassic time into previously extended crust. This magmatic activity accounts for a significant amount of crustal growth in the Andes, which is continuing at the present day.

7 North of Ecuador, in Colombia, crustal growth has switched in style between episodes of plutonism and episodes of terrane accretion. This part of South America has grown westwards as successive slivers tens of kilometres wide, such as the Amaime terrane, have been sheared onto the continental margin along strike–slip faults such as the Romeral Fault. The docking ages of these terranes lie between the youngest age of accreted terrane crust and the oldest age of plutons cutting the terrane boundary or the youngest age of sedimentary cover derived from adjacent (post-docking) crust.

8 Crustal growth results from arc magmatism when ocean lithosphere approaches an adjacent plate at a high angle ($> 25°$) and is therefore forced to subduct and then trigger magma generation in the mantle wedge. Terrane accretion is favoured by oblique ($< 25°$) convergence of oceanic lithosphere with a second plate. In this case, subduction is not feasible, so simultaneous terrane accretion and arc magmatism are mutually exclusive, as borne out by the geology of western Colombia.

9   The rate of crustal growth at arcs is estimated by dividing the geophysically estimated excess volume of crust by the duration of subduction. The average growth rate is 30 km^3 Ma^{-1} per km of arc. For the globe, this rate is equal to a total growth rate of 1.1 km^3 a^{-1}. This is a significant proportion of the average rate of crustal growth throughout Earth history, but can only account for two-thirds of the present volume of continental crust. Faster rates of crustal growth must have occurred in the Earth's earlier history.

SAQS FOR SECTION 5

SAQ 5.1   Decide whether each of the following is true or false.

(a) Plutons are often compositionally zoned from basic margins to acidic centres.

(b) Granitoids in subduction zones are typically peralkaline.

(c) Although oceanic island arc volcanoes usually erupt tholeiitic lavas, plutonic rocks in oceanic island arcs are always calc-alkaline.

(d) Estimates of the total present-day crustal growth rate at subduction zones are around 1.1 km^3 a^{-1}.

SAQ 5.2   What is the evidence that subduction zones are regions of crustal growth?

SAQ 5.3   Explain why the volume of volcanic rocks may (a) be an overestimate or (b) be an underestimate of the volume of magma input into the crust at subduction zones.

SAQ 5.4   Outline two methods that can be used to estimate the docking ages of displaced terranes.

SAQ 5.5   What has been the major difference between the styles of crustal growth in Colombia and Peru, and why have these differences arisen?

6   SUBDUCTION-RELATED GROWTH OF THE BRITISH ISLES

Our studies of modern subduction zones have shown the ways in which magmas and displaced terranes modify the geology of the crust and add material to it. Can we apply those ideas to the Lower Palaeozoic of the British Isles to understand the growth of our local crust? In Block 1A (Section 3.4), the geological history of the British Isles was shown to have involved the collision of northern and southern Britain along a tectonic join known as the Iapetus suture. This collision was the culmination of subduction processes along plate margins more than 400 million years ago that generated the Caledonian Orogenic Belt. Such spectacular conclusions are the outcome of detailed geological investigation at the local scale *and* the ability to view the large scale of plate tectonic processes. Modern convergent plate boundaries are much, much larger than the width of the British Isles for instance, so a proper understanding of British Caledonian geology has to take account of the geology of a much larger area. For instance, the British Caledonian rocks have counterparts in the Appalachians, Newfoundland, eastern Greenland, Svalbard (Spitzbergen), western Scandinavia, Germany and Poland (TMOE), so that on a pre-Atlantic reconstruction (Figure 6.1) these become joined into an orogenic zone with the shape of an inverted 'T' or 'Y'. On this large scale, the Caledonian orogeny requires the interaction of three plates—Laurentia, Baltica and a southern plate or plates such as the Avalonia and Cadomia terranes (Block 1A, Figure 3.29). Earlier models of the Caledonian Orogeny that relied on interactions between just two plates were clearly too simplified as they do not account for all of the observed geology. To get a more realistic understanding, we need to sort out the geological history of the plate boundaries, and this is made much easier by using the insights gained from observing present-day destructive margins in action. This Section carries some of the things we have learnt in this Block back to Palaeozoic times. We start by summarizing some key geological observations (some of which may be familiar to you from second level courses and from Block 1), and then interpret them in the context of present-day subduction zone processes.

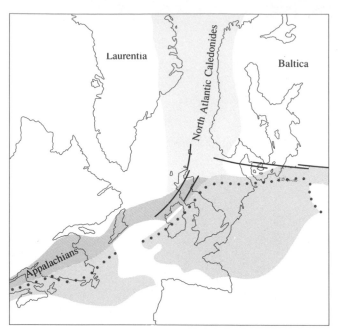

Figure 6.1 Pre-Atlantic reconstruction of Caledonian–Appalachian orogenic belts. Pale pink: N Atlantic Caledonides formed by collision of Laurentia and Baltica. Dark pink: Displaced terranes on the former southern margin of Laurentia. Dots: northern limit of southern terranes. Medium pink: deformation of late Caledonian and later age associated with the final orogenic deformation.

6.1 OBSERVATIONS

Since this Block is centred on the role of lithospheric processes at destructive margins, we focus on rocks formed at plate boundaries but now locked into the British crust.

> What types of geological feature can be found in the crust that identify the former presence of a nearby destructive margin?

Ophiolites, calc-alkaline igneous rocks and wedges of deep-sea trench sediments with structures similar to accretionary prisms are all to be found in the Lower Palaeozoic of the British Isles (Figure 6.2).

Ophiolites, or rather fragmentary associations of tholeiitic pillow basalt, chert, metashales and altered peridotite similar to those found in ophiolites, occur along the Highland Boundary Fault (the Highland Border Complex, also known as the Highland Border Series or Highland Boundary Complex), the Ballantrae–Girvan district north of the Southern Uplands Fault, and in County Tyrone and Clew Bay close to the western extrapolation of the Highland Boundary Fault (Figure 6.2). These bodies are of Lower Ordovician age—about 470 to 490 Ma.

> **ITQ 6.1** Locate the Highland Boundary Complex on the Tay Forth sheet (it is labelled in the key as HBX). What are the neighbouring rock types, and what are their field relationships to the HBX?

All of the above rock bodies have been emplaced tectonically, supporting their interpretation as ophiolite fragments that became incorporated into the crust at destructive plate margins.

Figure 6.2 Map of the British Isles showing the distribution of Lower Palaeozoic sediments, the Newer Granites, major faults and Lower Palaeozoic volcanics. Features mentioned in the text: B, Ballantrae ophiolite; C, Criffel pluton; CB, Clew Bay ophiolite; CT, County Tyrone ophiolite; CV, Cheviot volcanic and plutonic complex; L, Leinster pluton; LD, Loch Doon pluton; S, Shap pluton.

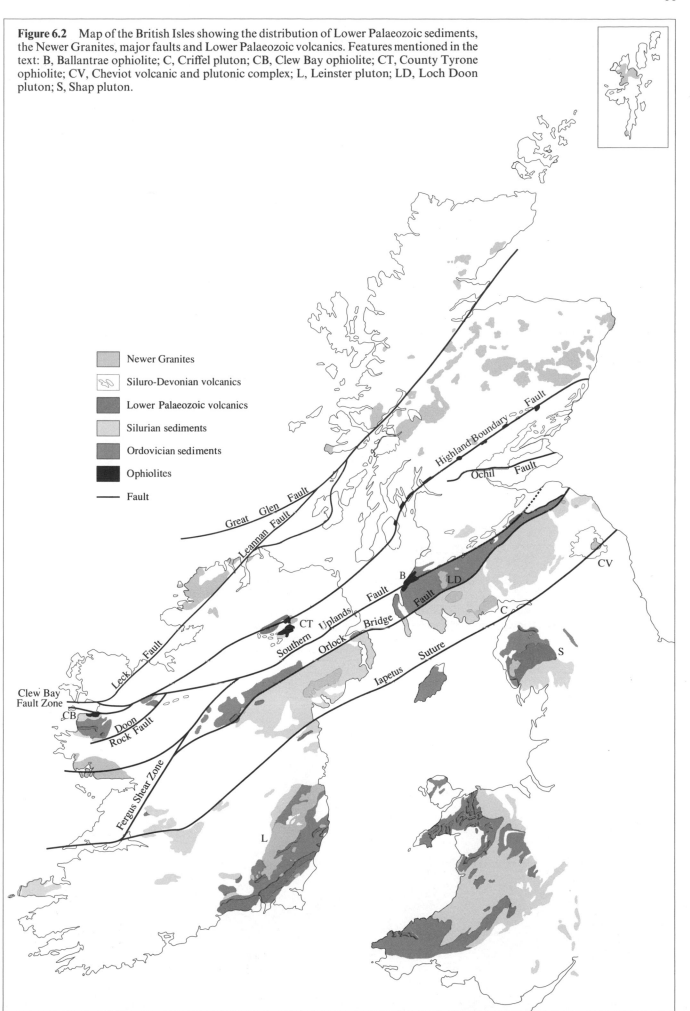

Newer Granites

Siluro-Devonian volcanics

Lower Palaeozoic volcanics

Silurian sediments

Ordovician sediments

Ophiolites

—— Fault

Great Glen Fault

Leannan Fault

Highland Boundary Fault

Ochil Fault

Leck Fault

Southern Uplands Fault

Orlock Bridge Fault

Iapetus Suture

Clew Bay Fault Zone

CB

Doon Rock Fault

Fergus Shear Zone

CT

B

LD

C

CV

S

L

82

As well as being able to see these fragments of ancient oceanic crust in the field, or on a geological map, your studies of geophysical maps in Block 1B, Section 2.3.1, revealed possibly more examples buried within the Southern Uplands Fault zone.

Instrusions and volcanics show great diversity. South of the Iapetus suture, Ordovician volcanics and Siluro-Devonian granitoids are found, while north of the suture, the igneous rocks are overwhelmingly Siluro-Devonian in age. These rocks give us an opportunity to investigate magmatic processes during Lower Palaeozoic subduction. One of the intrusions, the Loch Doon pluton (Figure 6.2) provides you with this opportunity as it forms the basis of the Home Kit exercise.

Before going on to Section 6.2, you should complete the Home Kit exercise; it is in two parts, each of which should take no more than one hour to complete. Better still, complete the exercise now.

Ordovician volcanics outcrop in three countries—England, Ireland and Wales (Figure 6.2). In the Lake District, the oldest lavas, the Eycott Volcanics, occur in the north, and comprise a tilted pile about 2.5 km thick. Individual lava flows can be as thick as 100 m and are mostly tholeiitic to calc-alkaline basalts and basaltic andesites. Further south, in the central Lake District, are the Borrowdale Volcanics, a thicker (*c.* 6 km) and slightly younger sequence that are generally calc-alkaline. Figures 6.3 and 6.4 show annotated views of the Lake District in the lower and upper parts of the Borrowdale Volcanics.

(a)

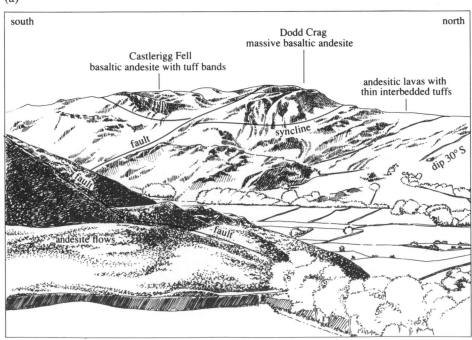

(b)

Figure 6.3 (a) View of Castlerigg Fell, 3 km southwest of Keswick, Cumbria, showing the lower part of the Borrowdale Volcanics. (b) Annotated sketch of (a).

(a)

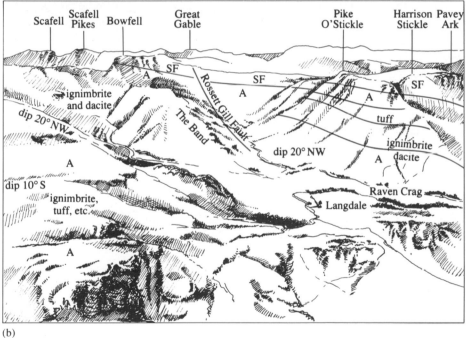

(b)

Figure 6.4 (a) View to the west north west across Langdale of Bowfell and the Langdale Pikes from Blea Tarn, Cumbria, showing the upper part of the Borrowdale Volcanics. (b) Annotated sketch of (a); Λ, Λiry's Bridge ignimbrite; SF, Seathwaite Fells Tuffs.

ITQ 6.2 What are the dominant magma compositions and eruptive style in (a) the lower Borrowdale Volcanics and (b) the upper Borrowdale Volcanics?

Although folding and faulting makes it difficult to trace out individual volcanic units, recent work has managed to demonstrate that the Airy's Bridge ignimbrite, which is seen in much of Figure 6.4 and marks the base of the Upper Borrowdale Volcanic Group, has a volume of at least 120 km³. It is very likely that such a huge eruption caused a collapse caldera to form. We must envisage that at least one calc-alkaline volcano, probably between Santorini (Figure 3.2) and Cerro Galan (CPB, Plate 3.4) in size, would have been active during the Ordovician in what is now the Lake District.

In Ireland, submarine volcanism was contemporaneous with submarine and sub-aerial eruptions in the Lake District. A northern belt can be distinguished from a southern belt (Figure 6.2). Compositional data from these two areas are given in Figure 6.5 and show that they are not identical.

ITQ 6.3 How do the north and south areas compare with respect to (a) tholeiitic versus calc-alkaline character, and (b) the range of rock types.

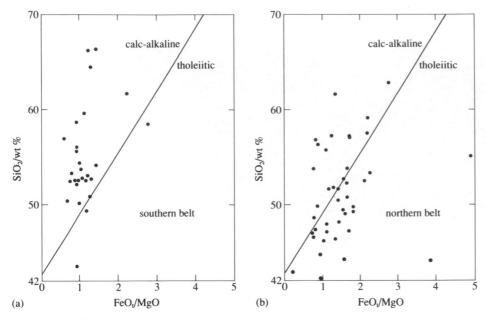

Figure 6.5 SiO$_2$ versus FeO$_t$/MgO plots for volcanic rocks in (a) the southern and (b) northern belt of Ordovician volcanics in southeastern Ireland.

So, as in the Lake District, there is a southward increase in silica content and the proportion of calc-alkaline to tholeiitic volcanics.

Ordovician volcanic rocks in Wales (Figure 6.2) range from tholeiitic, transitional and mildly alkaline basalts to calc-alkaline andesites, dacites and rhyolitic ignimbrites. It is difficult, if not impossible, to assign all of these rocks to a subduction-related origin. The alkaline magmas are more appropriate to a rifting environment, for instance (cf. Block 2).

The remaining igneous rocks shown on Figure 6.2 are all younger than 430 Ma. The basaltic andesite and andesite lavas of the Midland Valley are thus contemporaneous with the many granitoid plutons north of the Highland Boundary Fault, in Donegal, in the Southern Uplands and Longford–Down zone, and in the Lake District and Leinster. Many of the plutons are compositionally zoned from diorite to granite (e.g. Loch Doon, studied in the Home Kit exercise) and define coherent trends on variation diagrams, for example the AFM plot in Figure 6.6.

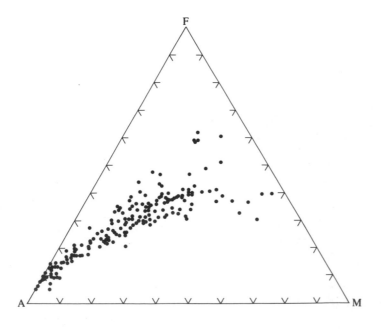

Figure 6.6 AFM plot of the Caledonian granitoids in Scotland younger than 430 Ma (the Newer Granites).

Do the data in Figure 6.6 describe a calc-alkaline or tholeiitic trend?

This suite of granitoids shows hardly any evidence of an iron-enrichment trend and can, therefore, be classed as calc-alkaline (Section 3.3.1) and their origin linked to subduction processes. These plutons are known as the **Newer Granites** because they were intruded after another phase of plutons (the **Older Granites**). The Older Granites have higher initial $^{87}Sr/^{86}Sr$ ratios indicative of a substantial proportion of remelted crust. They were also emplaced into rocks experiencing high metamorphic grades, while the Newer Granites were emplaced into cooler, brittle crust. The tectonic and thermal processes associated with the Older and Newer Granites were clearly different, and the crustal heating events that produced the Older Granites will be introduced in Block 4. The Scottish Newer Granites and contemporaneous calc-alkaline lavas on the other hand have a distinct subduction-related petrogenesis.

The youngest of the Newer Granites have ages close to 400 Ma. Most outcrop close to the Iapetus suture—in the southern parts of the Southern Uplands (e.g. Criffel, 397 Ma), the Lake District (e.g. Shap, 394 Ma) and southeast Ireland (e.g. Leinster, 404 Ma).

The final set of observations related to subduction concerns the evidence for an accretionary prism in the geology of the Ordovician and Silurian sediments in the Southern Uplands and its along-strike continuation in Ireland (Figure 6.2). The rocks comprise sequences of ocean floor basalt, chert and/or graptolitic shales, overlain by thick sequences of greywackes containing thin volcanic ash layers. At least ten of these successions have been mapped in the Southern Uplands, striking NE–SW subparallel with the Southern Uplands Fault and the Iapetus suture. The sequences are separated by reverse faults, such that within each sequence the rocks young to the NW, but across the Southern Uplands as a whole the youngest sequence is closest to England (Block 1A, Section 3.4.2, Figure 3.26). Present-day accretionary prisms show the same types of structures, and led us in Block 1A to conclude that the Ordovician and Silurian sedimentary sequences are preserved within a Palaeozoic accretionary prism formed by NW-directed subduction.

These are some of the larger pieces in the geological jigsaw puzzle of Palaeozoic plate tectonics. How can we use these pieces to understand the plate movements responsible for our present geology? Were the subduction zones like those of the Aegean, Peru or Colombia? Can we say when it all came to an end and England finally joined Scotland along the Iapetus suture? The next Section takes a leap into such speculative areas, but hopefully while keeping a grasp of the observed facts. Don't forget to do the Home Kit exercise now, if you have not already done it.

6.2 THE ORDOVICIAN VOLCANICS OF THE LAKE DISTRICT AND SOUTHEASTERN IRELAND

Earlier in this Block, you learned that the composition of arc magmas is loosely related to the type of crust—oceanic or continental, thick or thin—on which the magmatic arc lies. We can apply this result to ancient volcanic arcs such as the Ordovician volcanics in the Lake District and SE Ireland in order to discover the nature of the arc crust.

ITQ 6.4 Using the compositional information contained in Section 6.1, Figure 6.5 and discussed in ITQ 6.3, comment on the likelihood that Ordovician subduction occurred to the northwest or to the southeast.

The composition of these volcanic rocks allows us to identify the southern margin of the Iapetus Ocean. If the Lake District and SE Ireland were sites of activity along the volcanic front, then the Welsh magmatism must have belonged to either a second more southerly arc or be related to back-arc activity. The alkaline nature of some of the Welsh rocks is more in keeping with an extensional basin situated behind the arc.

6.3 SUBDUCTION AND PLATE MOVEMENT ALONG THE NORTHERN SHORE OF IAPETUS

The geology discussed in the last Section led to the well-accepted conclusion that subduction took place beneath the southern margin of Iapetus during the Ordovician (e.g. Block 1A, Figure 3.27). At the northern margin, things are not as simple. Northward subduction is indicated by the occurrence of Ordovician sediments in the Southern Uplands accretionary prism, but where are the Ordovician calc-alkaline volcanics and intrusions which should be in the Highlands?

> **ITQ 6.5**   At the present day, are there always volcanoes behind trenches at subduction zones?

From what we see at active plate boundaries today, it is possible to have subduction without magmas, so the lack of calc-alkaline rocks does not appear to be a problem. *However*, there are calc-alkaline ash layers in the accretionary prism, presumably blown offshore from an adjacent volcanic arc. So where have these ashes come from? More dramatically, where has the accretionary prism come from? The sediment has come from somewhere, and that source region can be identified by sedimentological studies. Current direction indicators (sedimentary structures such as cross-bedding) give the direction from which sediment entered the depositional site, and petrographic studies of individual clasts can identify the rock types in the eroded source area. These techniques form the basis of what are known as **provenance studies**. They are used to match up the source and depositional areas of sediments so that the palaeogeography of an area can be reconstructed.

Immediately south of the Southern Uplands Fault, a number of conglomerates within the Lower Ordovician turbidite sequence allow us to do some provenance studies of our own. The conglomerates formed in submarine fans as mass-flow deposits, and were transported in from the northwest carrying rounded granite boulders up to 1.5 m across. If these granites can be matched, on the basis of mineralogy, composition, texture and/or age, to some of the many pre-Ordovician granites in Scotland or Ireland, then we will have identified the source region of the conglomerates. Three types of granite boulder have been found:

1   foliated granite with an age of 1 200 Ma

2   undeformed granites in the range 600 to 700 Ma

3   deformed sodium-rich granite in the range 470 to 490 Ma.

Scottish or Irish granites older than about 1 000 Ma are unknown, as are granites in the age range 600 to 700 Ma. On the other hand, 470–490 Ma granites (the Older Granites) abound, but unlike those in the Southern Uplands conglomerates these are not sodium-rich. The inescapable conclusion is that the Ordovician sediments immediately south of the Southern Uplands Fault were not supplied from Scotland or Ireland—and yet the current directions still require a source to the northwest. Satisfactory matches for all three granite types can be found in northern Newfoundland. In order for boulders of these Canadian granites to end up in Southern Uplands conglomerates means that the two areas had been adjacent during the Lower Ordovician (Figure 6.7a). The Southern Uplands must then have slid northeast by about 1 500 km from an original position southeast of Newfoundland to its present location in southern Scotland (Figure 6.7b) (remember that the Atlantic Ocean did not exist in the Ordovician).

> **ITQ 6.6**   Can you suggest a possible fault or faults along which this sinistral movement could have been accommodated?

Sinistral movements along the Great Glen Fault, Highland Boundary Fault and Southern Uplands Fault together with other, minor NE–SW-striking faults in the Highlands and Ireland have been proposed in order to account for the evidence of large lateral displacements. These movements were more or less complete by the early Devonian, because by then, sediment sources and depositional areas can be matched on either side of the Southern Uplands Fault. The Southern Uplands are

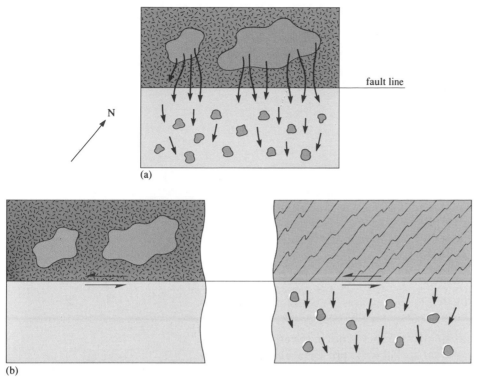

Figure 6.7 Cartoon maps of the sediment source and depositional areas on either side of a strike-slip fault. (a) Exposed plutons are providing sediment to a south-eastern area of deposition which lies beyond a strike-slip fault, building up strata that contain granitic clasts (red circles) and sedimentary structures that indicate transport from the northwest (short arrows). (b) Due to considerable sinistral fault movement, the sediments have been laterally displaced from their source. The sedimentary rocks record indications of southeastwards transport but the granite boulders have no counterpart to the northwest. This is the situation in the Lower Ordovician strata of the Southern Uplands.

thus concluded to be a displaced terrane, and this explains why a good deal of its sediments and volcanic ash have no obvious source in what are now its neighbouring areas.

ITQ 6.7 Detailed stratigraphic studies show that it took about 63 Ma for the Southern Uplands terrane to slide into its present position, adjacent to the Midland Valley. From what you know of the distance involved and the rates of present-day plate motions, are the geological inferences about the Southern Uplands' motion 'sensible'?

Strike–slip motion parallel to volcanic arcs and plate boundaries is well known. In Sumatra, for example, dextral slip parallel to the Sunda Trench occurs at about 3.6 cm a^{-1}. Provenance studies have shown that the Midland Valley is also likely to be a displaced terrane.

ITQ 6.8 Are there any other reasons for considering the basement of the Midland Valley to be a displaced terrane?

Ordovician to Devonian motion between the Highlands, Midland Valley and Southern Uplands involved many hundreds of kilometres of largely lateral displacement. Apparently fragments of Ordovician oceanic crust became squeezed in between the glancing terranes and formed the ophiolite fragments adjacent to the Highland Boundary and Southern Uplands Faults. Similar relationships are found in rocks of roughly the same age in Newfoundland (Block 1A, Figure 3.19), with the result that the continental mass of Laurasia on the northern shore of Iapetus is inferred to have grown by the accretion of several terranes of arc-related crustal slivers and intervening ophiolite fragments.

6.4 THE IAPETUS SUTURE AND THE END OF SUBDUCTION

The evidence for the existence of Iapetus has come from the rocks interpreted to have formed along its margins. When did Iapetus disappear and its shores become locked together along the Iapetus suture? The date of this event will be between the youngest pre-collision event and the oldest post-collision event. This technique allowed us to date the accretion events in Colombia (Section 5.3.2) by studying the timing of granite emplacement. Radiometric dating, using the Rb/Sr method, provides precise ages, so all that is needed are the right rocks to date! The plutons and lavas provide the best material for dating and they can be assigned to pre- or post-collision emplacement on the basis of their compositional affinities.

Thus the lavas and Newer Granites in the Highlands, Midland Valley and the northern part of the Southern Uplands (i.e. within 25 km of the Southern Uplands Fault, e.g. the Loch Doon pluton) can be assigned as pre-collisional, because they share calc-alkaline characteristics similar to those of present day subduction zone magmas. All of these rocks are older than 408 Ma.

In the rest of the Southern Uplands and in the Lake District, the granitoids are compositionally distinct from those further north, and thus form a separate group most of which date from 400 to 392 Ma. Although still calc-alkaline, there are problems in explaining how this set of granites lying on either side of the Iapetus suture (Figure 6.2) can be related to a single destructive margin. A 'new' subduction zone would have to be invented, but nobody has found any other evidence to support this idea yet. A more likely conclusion is that these distinctive granites which straddle the suture were contemporaneous with or after the collision. The lavas and related intrusions of the Cheviot Hills (Figure 6.2 and CPB, Plates 1.1 and 1.2) lie virtually on top of the suture. This 'Cheviot volcano', dated at 396 Ma must have been active after Iapetus had closed. The collision event must have taken place between 408 and 396 Ma—a little later than the Silurian–Devonian boundary which is defined at 412 Ma.

Recall that the suture is a deep structure, geophysically detectable to depths of over 30 km (Block 1B, and video VC 271, *Fragments of Britain*). The present erosion level exposes the upper roots of volcanoes that would have been just a few kilometres beneath the Silurian-Devonian land surface. You cannot stand on the suture in the field. If we want to see what a collision zone looks like and find out which tectonic, magmatic and metamorphic processes occur there, it is necessary to study deeper parts of the crust. That is the mission of Block 4 *Continental compression*.

Summary

Although elements of modern subduction zones such as accretionary prisms, ophiolites and calc-alkaline igneous rocks have been recognized in the British Caledonides for over two decades, it has taken more recent analyses of subduction zone processes (Sections 2–5) to start reconstructing satisfactory pictures of how Lower Palaeozoic subduction relates to the generation of the British lithosphere. The events associated with the northern margin of the Iapetus Ocean are perhaps best understood. At this plate margin, sinistral movements of up to 1 500 km have been invoked to explain the evidence from regional geophysical anomalies, lower crustal xenoliths and sedimentary petrology (provenance studies) that the Midland Valley and Southern Uplands are displaced terranes. Closure of the Iapetus Ocean, along the Iapetus suture, occurred between 408 and 396 Ma ago.

SAQS FOR SECTION 6

SAQ 6.1 What is the evidence to suggest that (a) the Southern Uplands is a displaced terrane and that (b) it experienced sinistral movement prior to its docking?

SAQ 6.2 What is the basis for stating that the Iapetus suture formed some time between 408 and 396 Ma?

ITQ ANSWERS AND COMMENTS

ITQ 2.1 In most cases, h is a little over 100 km. To a good approximation, the individual depths for each subduction zone are: North Chile (NC), 120 km; Kurile/Kamchatka (KK) and Tonga (T), 100 km; Kermadec (KER) and New Zealand (NZ), 105 km; Izu-Bonin (IB), 120 km; Aleutians (ALT), Alaska (ALK) and Mariana (M), 110 km; Central America (CA), 140 km; New Hebrides (NH), 190 km.

ITQ 2.2 (a) Using $P = \rho gh$ with $\rho = 3.3 \times 10^3$ kg m^{-3} and $g = 10$ m s^{-2} gives $P \approx 3$ GPa ($= 30$ kbar) for $h = 90$ km (9×10^4 m) and $P \approx 4.3$ GPa ($= 43$ kbar) for $h = 130$ km.

(b) These pressures are somewhat greater than those at which amphibolite dehydrates (25 to 30 kbar).

ITQ 3.1 (a) Although the occasional point strays across the drawn boundaries, the Skaros rocks belong to a medium-K series (Group II).

(b) Samples 181 and 180 are basalts, 182 and 178 are basaltic-andesites, 171 is an andesite, and 153 is a dacite.

ITQ 3.2 (a) According to Figure 3.11, no lavas with less than about 55% SiO$_2$ contain magnetite. Similarly none with more than about 58% SiO$_2$ contain olivine. So, the switch from plagioclase + augite + olivine-bearing lavas to plagioclase + augite + orthopyroxene + magnetite-bearing lavas occurs in the range 55–58% SiO$_2$.

(b) In Figure 3.8, the boundary between basaltic andesites and andesites occurs at SiO$_2 = 56\%$. Thus, there are consistent chemical and mineralogical differences between these two rock types.

ITQ 3.3 (a) By the definition, Mg ratio $= 100 \times$ En/(En + Fs). We have an Mg ratio for this crystal of $100 \times 47.1/(47.1 + 12.4) = 79.2$.

(b) The approximate composition is En$_{38}$Fs$_{22}$Wo$_{40}$, giving an Mg ratio of 63.3. Note that the En, Fs and Wo contents should total 100.

ITQ 3.4 (a) As the Al$_2$O$_3$ content of the basalt and andesite are about the same, i.e. c. 18.5%, the extract must also have c. 18.5% Al$_2$O$_3$. If this were not the case, the fractionated liquid would have a different Al$_2$O$_3$ content. For example, removal of only olivine, which contains no Al$_2$O$_3$, from the basalt would produce liquids with more than 18.5% Al$_2$O$_3$.

(b) Plagioclase has 29 to 35% Al$_2$O$_3$, while olivine and augite have hardly any (0 and 1–4%, respectively). A mineral assemblage with 18.5% Al$_2$O$_3$ must, therefore, contain a lot of plagioclase. To a rough approximation, 50 to 60% plagioclase and 50 to 40% olivine + augite would have about the requisite amount of alumina.

(c) At c. 57% SiO$_2$, the Al$_2$O$_3$ content of the lavas start to decrease with increasing SiO$_2$ instead of staying constant, as was the case for lavas with less than 57% SiO$_2$. This would be possible if the composition of the mineral extract changed significantly at 57% SiO$_2$. This is a likely possibility, as we have previously established (Figure 3.11) that the mineral assemblage in the lavas changes from plagioclase + augite + olivine at SiO$_2 < c$. 57% to plagioclase + augite + orthopyroxene + magnetite at SiO$_2 > c$. 57%.

ITQ 3.5 (a) According to equation 3.6, we have

$$D_{Ni} = X_{plag}K_{D,plag} + X_{aug}K_{D,aug} + X_{ol}K_{D,ol}$$

and substituting the given values for the X and K_D terms

$$D_{Ni} = 0.6 \times 0.01 + 0.1 \times 2.0 + 0.3 \times 6.2$$

$$D_{Ni} = 0.006 + 0.2 + 1.86$$

$$D_{Ni} = 2.066$$

(b) According to the definition of the bulk partition coefficient (equation 3.5) and the result $D_{Ni} = 2.066$, the concentration of Ni in the mineral assemblage will be just over twice that in the coexisting liquid.

ITQ 3.6 See completed table below (Table A1).

Table A1 Normalized liquid composition C_l/C_o as a function of the fraction of liquid remaining F, during Rayleigh fractionation with bulk partition coefficient D.

F	$D = 3$	$D = 2$	$D = 1$	$D = 0$
1	1.00	1.00	1.00	1.00
0.9	0.81	0.90	1.00	1.11
0.8	0.64	0.80	1.00	1.25
0.7	0.49	0.70	1.00	1.43
0.6	0.36	0.60	1.00	1.67
0.5	0.25	0.50	1.00	2.00
0.4	0.16	0.40	1.00	2.50
0.3	0.09	0.30	1.00	3.33
0.2	0.04	0.20	1.00	5.00
0.1	0.01	0.10	1.00	10.00

ITQ 3.7 See completed figure below (Figure A1).

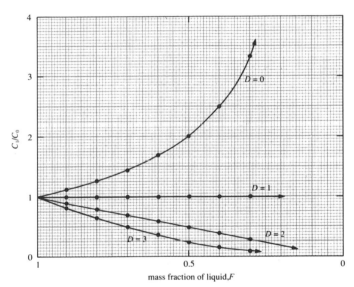

Figure A1 Completed Figure 3.16 (see ITQ 3.7).

ITQ 3.8 (a) Here $C_o = 5$ p.p.m. and $C_l = 16$ p.p.m., so

$$16 = 5\, F^{D_{Rb}-1} = 5F^{-1} = 5/F \text{ hence } F = 5/16 = 0.312\,5$$

That is, of the original basalt, 68.75% has been removed as a mixture of plagioclase, augite and olivine crystals to leave 31.25% of andesite. Alternatively, using Figure A1, $C_l/C_o = 3.2$, so $F = 0.31$ can be read using the curve for $D = 0$.

(b) In this case $C_o = 100$, and we are required to find C_l, using $C_l = C_o F^{D-1}$.
From part (a), $F = 0.312\,5$ and $D_{Ni} = 2.0$, so

$$C_l = 100\,(0.312\,5)^{2-1} = 100 \times 0.312\,5 = 31.25$$

The andesite should contain 31.25 p.p.m. Ni according to the Rayleigh fractionation equation. Again this result can be found graphically, from Figure A1, with $F = 0.31$ and the $D = 2$ curve to give $C_l/C_o = 0.31$, which, with $C_o = 100$ p.p.m., gives $C_l = 31$ p.p.m. This is in accord with the calculation using Rb in (a), so we can conclude that fractional crystallization according to the Rayleigh equation is the process that links the andesite to the basalt.

ITQ 3.9 See completed figure below (Figure A2).

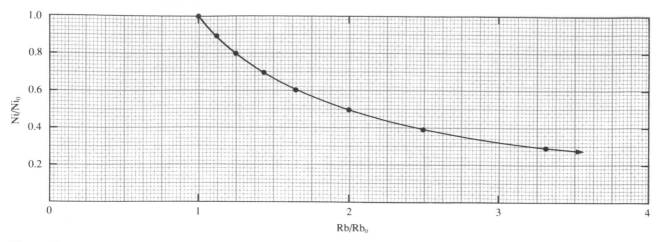

Figure A2 Completed Figure 3.17 (see ITQ 3.9).

ITQ 3.10 Only those compositions that formed by fractional crystallization from this particular basalt will have Ni/Ni_o and Rb/Rb_o ratios that plot on the curve you constructed in Figure 3.17. The Ni/Ni_o and Rb/Rb_o ratios of rocks A to D are thus 0.71 and 1.4 for A, 0.5 and 2 for B, 0.45 and 2.6 for C, and 0.89 and 1.4 for D. Of these, only A and B plot on the curve of Figure 3.17. C and D are not related to this parental basalt by fractional crystallization.

ITQ 3.11 The gradient of the straight line is determined using a ruler, not by reading off trace element abundances on the x (horizontal) and y (vertical) axes. Thus, from Figure 3.18b, the gradient in this case is (see Figure A3) the measured vertical distance divided by the measured horizontal distance, i.e. -1.

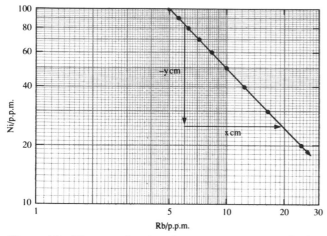

Figure A3 Diagram showing the measurements required to determine the slope of a line.

ITQ 3.12 The bulk partition coefficient is a function of the minerals present, their proportions, and their individual K_D values (equation 3.6). A difference in any of these parameters between two magmas will result in different bulk partition coefficients (unless K_D is the same for every mineral—this possibility occurs with highly incompatible elements, i.e. those with $K_D = 0$ for every mineral).

ITQ 3.13 (a) The Th contents must be in the middle of the range 6.4 to 12.4 p.p.m., presumably around 8 to 10 p.p.m.

(b) The break of slope in the log–log variation diagrams occur at about 10 p.p.m. Th—a close match with the answer in part (a).

ITQ 3.14 The slopes of the trends are, -0.14 for V, -0.19 for Sc and 0.0 for Sr. (Do not be concerned if you got slightly different values—everyone's use of a ruler is not precisely identical!) Using $D_{Th} = 0$ and equation 3.12 then gives $D_V = 1.14$, $D_{Sc} = 1.19$ and $D_{Sr} = 1.0$.

ITQ 3.15 From equation 3.20, $X_{plagioclase} = 1.0/1.9 = 0.53$. Equations 3.19 and 3.21 give two answers for X_{augite}; the answer using the equation for Sc is $1.19/4.2 = 0.28$ and for V is $1.14/3.8 = 0.30$, giving an average of 0.29. $X_{olivine}$ can then be found from equation 3.18: $6.2X_{olivine} = 1.69 - 2X_{augite} = 1.11$, so $X_{olivine} = 1.11/6.2 = 0.18$. The proportions (by mass) of plagioclase, augite and olivine in the fractionating assemblage are thus 0.53, 0.29 and 0.18 respectively. (If you used slightly different numbers from those given in the answer to ITQ 3.14, then you may have got slightly different answers for this ITQ.)

ITQ 3.16 For the basalt, $Ce_N = 17$ and $Yb_N = 8.5$, giving $(Ce/Yb)_N = 2$ (don't worry if you read off slightly different values from Figure 3.22; as long as you found Ce_N to be a little less than 20 and Yb_N a little less than 10, then there is no problem, and your value of $(Ce/Yb)_N$ should have been close to 2). Similarly for the andesite $(Ce/Yb)_N = 65/20 = 3.25$.

ITQ 3.17 From Figure 3.23, the partition coefficient for Eu between plagioclase and liquid is about five times greater than the partition coefficients for Sm and Gd between plagioclase and liquid. When plagioclase is a fractionating mineral, Eu will be more compatible than Sm and Gd, resulting in less enrichment of Eu in the differentiated magmas.

ITQ 3.18 Careful measurements in reading off the values from Figure 3.22 should show

(a) $Eu/Eu^* = 10.5/11.2 = 0.94$;

(b) $Eu/Eu^* = 15.5/20.5 = 0.76$;

(c) $Eu/Eu^* = 19.5/27 = 0.72$.

(Don't worry if you made slightly different readings; your results should turn out roughly the same.)

ITQ 3.19 The greater the negative europium anomaly, i.e. the smaller Eu/Eu^*, the greater is the amount of plagioclase fractionation. Thus the andesite is more fractionated than the basaltic andesite, and this accords with all our earlier work.

ITQ 3.20 To produce a mixed magma with olivine, orthopyroxene and magnetite crystals requires an olivine-bearing magma to be mixed with an orthopyroxene- and magnetite-bearing magma. Those end-members have, respectively, less than about 55% SiO_2 (i.e. basalt or basaltic andesite) and more than about 55% SiO_2 (i.e. andesite or dacite).

ITQ 3.21 (a) The Mg ratios are respectively $100 \times 47/(47 + 9) = 83.9$ and $100 \times 43/(43 + 18) = 70.5$. Figure 3.14 implies that these crystals grew from magmas with about 6.5 to 7.5% MgO and 1 to 4% MgO.

(b) The olivine composition may have grown from a magma with about 7.5% MgO.

(c) The more calcic plagioclase most probably grew from basalt ($<52\%$ SiO_2) or basaltic andesite ($52–56\%$ SiO_2). The sodic plagioclase most probably grew from andesite ($56–63\%$ SiO_2) or dacite ($>63\%$ SiO_2).

ITQ 4.1 Seismic refraction studies identify the interfaces between rock layers with different seismic velocities and also establish the seismic velocities of the layers themselves. The seismic velocities of a rock (e.g. v_P) are a function of its density and elastic moduli, which are in turn related to its chemical composition and mineralogy.

ITQ 4.2 (a) No, layers with discrete ranges of seismic velocities are identified in all of the crustal sections.

(b) The upper layer ($v_P = 5.0$ to 5.7 kms^{-1}) is about 1.5 km thick in oceanic crust, but 6 to 8 km thick at island arcs. The lower crustal layer (6.5 to 7.0 $km\,s^{-1}$) is also thicker in island arc crust (6 to 18 km) than in normal ocean crust ($c.$ 4 km).

(c) Three layers are defined within continental crust on the basis of P-wave velocities; they are also present in all but one example of an active continental margin. The uppermost layer is about 10 km in the continental interior, but can be half this thickness at an active margin. In contrast, the lowermost layer is thicker at the active margins (20 to 45 km) than in the continental interior ($c.$ 18 km). The middle layer ($v_P = 5.8$ to 6.2 $km\,s^{-1}$) has variable thickness, and can be absent or 1.5 times as thick as in the continental interior, where it is 15 km thick.

(d) Active continental margins differ from island arcs in having thicker crust. The former comprises three layers, while island arcs generally have two crustal layers. The upper layers are of about the same thickness (6 to 10 km) in both areas, but the lower layer is thicker in active continental margins.

(e) The uppermost parts of most mantle wedges have slightly lower v_P than the mantle beneath oceanic and continental interiors.

(f) The presence of a liquid phase reduces v_P, and in volcanic arcs, reduced mantle v_P values are attributed to the existence of partial melt in the mantle wedge.

ITQ 4.3 (a) Volcanoes occur in four regions only (Figure 4.2a). These lie between latitudes of 5° N and 2° S (in Colombia and Ecuador), 16° and 28° S (mainly southern Peru and northern Chile), 31° and 46° S (central Chile), and 49° and 54° S (in southern Chile). These are referred to as the Northern Volcanic Zone (NVZ), Central Volcanic Zone (CVZ), Southern Volcanic Zone (SVZ) and Austral Volcanic Zone (AVZ) respectively and you should label Figure 4.2a accordingly.

(b) The spacing of contours on the Benioff Zone (Figure 4.2a) shows it to vary in dip along the length of the Andes, being relatively steep (in fact about 30°) in areas containing volcanoes. Cross-sections (Figure 4.2b) beneath central Peru and northern Chile also demonstrate the very different dips of the slab in these two areas. Note that a volcanic arc is lacking in central Peru, where the dip of the slab is relatively slight.

(c) The oldest oceanic lithosphere entering the Peru–Chile Trench is Eocene in age (Figures 4.2c), which subducts beneath southern Peru and northern Chile. To the north and south of this area, subducting lithosphere becomes younger, the most youthful being recently created lithosphere produced at the Chile Rise spreading centre. The Nazca and Juan Fernandez Ridges (Figure 4.2a) are very large topographic highs on the ocean floor approaching the Peru–Chile Trench.

(d) Along the entire length of the Andes, the crust is seldom less than 30 km thick. The thickest crust is found in Peru, Bolivia, northwest Argentina and northern Chile, where thicknesses of up to 70 km exist (Figure 4.2d).

(e) The most complex region of Andean basement is in western Colombia and Ecuador, where strips of Tertiary, Cretaceous, and Palaeozoic basement run parallel to the plate margin (Figure 4.2c). From near the Ecuador–Peru border (5° S), south to $c.$ 30° S, the basement is Precambrian. Further south still, the basement is Palaeozoic.

ITQ 4.4 (a) Compatible trace elements are those with $D > 1$ due to the presence of minerals with $K_D \gg 1$ in the crystallizing assemblage. The D value for one compatible trace element is thus very likely to be different from that of another.

(b) Incompatible trace elements have $D < 1$ due to the presence of minerals with $K_D < 1$ (although small proportions of a mineral with $K_D > 1$ can also be present in an assemblage for which $D < 1$). Elements for which $K_D \ll 1$ are said to be highly incompatible, and they have essentially identical K_D, and hence D, values of approximately 0.

ITQ 4.5 The rocks of Puyehue volcano have the same $^{87}Sr/^{86}Sr$ ratio, irrespective of their SiO_2 content. This can be explained by fractional crystallization of basalt to produce all of the other lavas and/or mixing between high- and low-SiO_2 magmas with identical strontium isotope ratios.

At Cerro Galan and Lascar $^{87}Sr/^{86}Sr$ increases with SiO_2, and this cannot be caused by fractional crystallization. The more silicic magmas at these volcanoes must have been contaminated by rocks or magma with higher $^{87}Sr/^{86}Sr$ than the more basic magmas.

ITQ 4.6 The ratio of incompatible trace elements in the magmas are useful in trying to discern crustal contamination. A plot of two highly incompatible trace elements will define a straight line only if the magmas have not been contaminated by material with a different ratio of the two plotted trace elements.

ITQ 4.7 On Figure 4.10, the Cerro Galan rocks define a curved trend and so cannot be solely accounted for by mixing crust and basalt in varying proportions, so contamination by thermal erosion cannot be a major process at this volcano.

ITQ 4.8 (a) (i) and (ii) Since silicic crust has higher $^{87}Sr/^{86}Sr$ and Rb/Sr than basalt, crustal contamination must lead to an increase of both these ratios within the magma.

(b) (i) During fractional crystallization, isotope ratios do not change (Section 4.3.2) so $^{87}Sr/^{86}Sr$ remains constant. Examples of this occur at Santorini (Figure 4.4b) and Puyehue (Figure 4.5). (ii) Rb is an incompatible trace element, while Sr is a compatible trace element (Section 3.4.2). Thus, Rb increases during fractional crystallization, while Sr decreases. Consequently Rb/Sr increases during fractional crystallization.

ITQ 4.9 The rock with Rb/Sr $= 0.39$ and $^{87}Sr/^{86}Sr = 0.70488$ plots below the curved (AFC) trend defined by all the other rocks. It has an unusually high Rb/Sr ratio compared to other lavas at this volcano with the same $^{87}Sr/^{86}Sr$. Fractional crystallization of magma with Rb/Sr of 0.1 or less would give a magma with higher Rb/Sr but unchanged $^{87}Sr/^{86}Sr$ (cf. the black evolution paths on Figure 4.13). The rock has an unusual composition in comparison with other Marmolejo rocks—a feature that reflects an unusual lack of contamination in its evolution. (This could be due to it having evolved in a part of a magma chamber that was isolated from readily melted country rock).

ITQ 5.1 (a) Granite has a higher quartz/feldspar ratio than quartz monzonite.

(b) Tonalite has a lower alkali feldspar/plagioclase ratio than granodiorite.

(c) Granite has a higher alkali feldspar/plagioclase than granodiorite.

(d) Granodiorite has higher quartz/feldspar ratio and higher alkali feldspar/plagioclase ratio than quartz diorite.

(e) Gabbro, which has a low modal quartz content, has a lower quartz/feldspar ratio than quartz diorite.

ITQ 5.2 (a) Most of the rocks from Finger Bay have less than 60% SiO_2; the opposite is true for those from Senal Blanca. The island arc example is thus less silicic than that from the continental margin.

(b) With reference to Figure 3.9, the island arc pluton is tholeiitic, while the continental margin pluton is calc-alkaline.

(c) Quartz is more abundant in the (more silicic) rocks of Senal Blanca than in those of Finger Bay. Granites, granodiorites and tonalites are found at Senal Blanca, while Finger Bay contains gabbros, diorites, quartz diorite, quartz monzodiorite and quartz monzonite.

ITQ 5.3 (a) The geological boundaries and the cordillera trend roughly NNE–SSW, so the maximum variation in geology is best seen on an east–west traverse across the country.

(b) Progressing from east to west, the rocks become younger, changing from the Precambrian and Palaeozoic of the Eastern Cordillera through Mesozoic to Tertiary ocean floor and overlying sediments in the Coastal Cordillera.

(c) East of the Romeral Fault Zone, the basement is made from crystalline igneous and metamorphic rocks. West of the fault zone, ocean floor igneous rocks form the basement.

(d) Plutons in the Central Cordillera are Mesozoic and those of the Western Cordillera are Tertiary, so the youngest plutons are in the west of the country.

ITQ 5.4 Plutons of episode C (Cretaceous, 125 to 70 Ma) cut the Romeral Fault at latitudes 7° N and 5.5° N. Upper Tertiary plutons (episode E—30 to 0 Ma) cut the fault at 5° and 1.5° N.

ITQ 5.5 As given in Section 5.2, the Coastal Batholith of Peru has a volume of 10^6 km³ and was emplaced over 70 Ma, giving an average rate of intrusion into the crust of about 14.3×10^3 km³ Ma⁻¹ (or 14.3×10^{-3} km³ a⁻¹).

ITQ 5.6 The intrusion rate of the Coastal Batholith was 14.3×10^3 km³ Ma⁻¹ (from ITQ 5.5), and it is 1 600 km long (Section 5.2). This gives an intrusion rate of $14.3 \times 10^3/1600 = 9$ km³ Ma⁻¹ km⁻¹.

ITQ 5.7 (a) The rate of growth is 30 km³ Ma⁻¹ km⁻¹ × 37 000 km = 1.1 km³ a⁻¹. (b) The long-term growth rate is $7.8 \times 10^9/4.55 \times 10^9 = 1.7$ km³ a⁻¹.

ITQ 6.1 The Highland Boundary Complex (HBX) is in contact with Dalradian metasediments to the northwest and Devonian sediments and volcanics to the southeast. All of the contacts between the HBX and its neighbours are faults. These faults cut across lithological boundaries in the Dalradian and Devonian successions.

ITQ 6.2 (a) The lower Borrowdales are mainly basaltic andesites and andesite lava flows; pyroclastic rocks are subordinate. (b) In the upper Borrowdales, silicic rocks (dacite) are common and occur as thick layers of tuff and ignimbrite.

ITQ 6.3 (a) In the northern belt, some rocks are calc-alkaline, while others are tholeiitic. In the southern belt, they are virtually all calc-alkaline. (b) Rocks from the northern belt range from basalt with very low silica to andesite. In the southern belt, most of the rocks are basalts or basaltic andesites, but rocks as silicic as dacite are also present.

ITQ 6.4 Tholeiitic volcanics (Eycott volcanics and the Northern Belt in Ireland) at subduction zones are usually associated with thin, oceanic crust. The submarine nature of many of these volcanics is compatible with their eruption in an oceanic volcanic arc. Calc-alkaline volcanics (Borrowdale volcanics and the Southern Belt in Ireland) are more usually associated with thicker, continental, crust. In the Lake District and southeastern Ireland, the Ordovician magmas become more calc-alkaline and silicic to the southeast, implying thickening of the crust in that direction, away from the plate edge. This in turn implies that subduction beneath the volcanic arc was to the southeast.

ITQ 6.5 No, magmas fail to be generated if the downgoing slab is not dense enough to sink into the mantle (Section 4.2) or if the ocean plate approaches at an oblique angle (Section 5.3.3).

ITQ 6.6 The most obvious candidate is the Southern Uplands Fault, as this forms the northern margin of the Southern Uplands accretionary prism.

ITQ 6.7 Displacement over 1 500 km during 63 Ma implies a translation speed of $1 500 \times 10^5/63 \times 10^6 = 2.4$ cm a⁻¹. This is similar to present-day speeds (see, for example, Block 1A, Figure 3.3) so the conclusions about the Southern Uplands movement are compatible with the mechanics of plate motion.

ITQ 6.8 Geophysically, the Midland Valley is distinct from the Highlands in having higher Bouguer gravity anomalies (see the large coloured Bouguer gravity anomaly map of Britain that accompanies Block 1B). The density difference between Highland and Midland Valley basement that this implies can be considered as evidence that the two regions have distinct crustal properties. In other words, the Midland Valley basement is not a southern extension of the Highlands. This is compatible with the idea that the Midland Valley is a separate terrane.

A second piece of evidence for this idea comes from samples of lower Midland Valley crust brought to the surface in Carboniferous volcanic vents (Block 2). These have more similarities with present-day Canadian basement than with that of northern Scotland, indicating that the Highlands and the Midland Valley are crustal blocks with separate histories, i.e. terranes.

SAQ ANSWERS AND COMMENTS

SAQ 2.1 (a) False. Although andesites are very commonly erupted in volcanic arcs, more primitive basalts are also found, and being primitive provide better candidates for the composition of primary magma.

(b) False. The presence of hydrous alteration minerals (clay minerals and chlorite) in the upper parts of oceanic lithosphere means that subducted ocean floor basalt will not be dry.

(c) True. The upper surface of the slab is detected by the positions of earthquake foci that define the Benioff zone. Beneath most volcanic arcs, this is at a depth of 90 to 130 km (Figures 2.4, 2.5), equivalent to pressures of 30 to 43 kbar.

(d) False. The solidus temperature of wet basalt is lower than that of dry basalt (Figure 2.2a).

(e) False. On the phase diagram of Figure 2.2a, the curve denoting the P–T conditions at which amphibolite transforms to eclogite + water is almost parallel with the temperature axis when $P \approx 25$ kbar.

(f) False. For the conditions along typical subduction zone geotherms (Figure 2.2a), the amphibolite to eclogite reaction occurs at sub-solidus temperatures, so no silicate melt is produced. The products of the reaction are eclogite (pyroxene, garnet, SiO_2) and water-rich fluid.

SAQ 2.2 (a) Andesite; (b) basalt.

SAQ 2.3 If frictional heating along the slab/mantle wedge interface leads to melting, then rapidly subducting slabs should create magmas after having subducted for only a short distance. The speed of subduction and trench–arc distance are, therefore, the appropriate parameters with which to test the frictional heating model. (As found from Figure 2.1, the available data do not support this mechanism of magma genesis.)

SAQ 2.4 The slab will melt if it can reach temperatures above the slab's solidus at a pressure less than that required for slab dehydration. This requires a shallow geotherm along the slab, and a high water content in the slab (needed to give a low solidus temperature). The observation that the primary magmas in arcs are basalt, the partial melting product of mantle peridotite, rather than andesite, the partial melting product of hydrous basalt, implies that slab melting is at most insignificant, and therefore, that the physical and chemical conditions required for the slab to melt are not reached within subduction zones.

SAQ 3.1 (a) True; this feature is seen in the sharp rise in FeO_t/MgO with SiO_2 in Figure 3.9, and the arched fractionation trend that rises towards the F (FeO_t) apex on an AFM plot (Figure 3.10).

(b) False; it is usually found that medium-K magma series are described as calc-alkaline using the definitions of Figures 3.9 and 3.10. Low-K arc magmas tend to be tholeiitic, although the degree of iron-enrichment is not as pronounced as in ocean basalts (e.g. Iceland, which is shown in Figures 3.9 and 3.10, and MORB).

(c) True; for example in Figures 3.12 and 3.14, the proportion of the Mg end member in olivine and augite in Santorini magmas is seen to decrease with decreasing MgO (increasing fractionation) in the magma.

(d) False; fractionated calc-alkaline magmas are always poorer in iron than their parent magmas, so magma density decreases with fractionation.

SAQ 3.2 (a) The Mg ratio of a pyroxene is $100 \times En/(Fs + En)$, so the Mg ratios here are, in increasing order, B (73.6), A (77.8) and C (83.3).

(b) The highest Mg ratios should be in equilibrium with the most primitive magmas. Here, pyroxene C is typical of that found in basalts at Santorini (Figures 3.13 and 3.14).

SAQ 3.3 (a) To calculate the mass of liquid remaining from the compositions of parent (181) and daughter (153) magmas and the bulk partition coefficient requires the use of the Rayleigh fractionation equation (equation 3.7). Here $C_1 = 16.0$, $C_o = 1.1$, $D = 0$, and we wish to find F. Thus, $16.0 = 1.1 F^{D-1} = 1.1 F^{-1}$.

$16.0/1.1 = 1/F$
$F = 1.1/16.0 = 0.069$

The mass fraction remaining is 0.069 (or 6.9%).

(b) The bulk partition coefficient depends on the mineral partition coefficients (K_D) and proportions of the fractionating minerals (X) (equation 3.6). For Th, K_D is very small, i.e. very close to zero, for all minerals (Table 3.4), so no matter what the proportions of the minerals, $D_{Th} \approx 0$.

SAQ 3.4 (a) From the definition of the Rayleigh fractionation equation, the slope of a straight line fractionation trend on a log–log plot of Sr (vertical axis) against Th (horizontal axis) is $m = (D_{Sr} - 1)/(D_{Th} - 1)$. For the evolved magmas in Figure 3.20, $m = -1.3$. So, with $D_{Th} = 0$, then $-1.3 = (D_{Sr} - 1)/-1$, giving $D_{Sr} = 1.3 + 1 = 2.3$.

(b) D_{Sr} depends on the minerals present—their proportions and their K_D values. Thus the different $D_{Sr}(= 1)$ in the more primitive magmas implies some combination of (i) different mineralogy or (ii) the same mineralogy but with either different proportions of the minerals, or different mineral K_D values (K_D^{Sr} between plagioclase and liquid tends to be higher for evolved magmas than in primitive magmas).

SAQ 3.5 (a) The maximum amounts of compositional variation are required in order to identify and distinguish the effects of fractional crystallization. Th and Rb are equally incompatible; their concentrations in rock E are fifteen times those in rock A. Sr remains essentially constant throughout the magma series. Ni is compatible: its concentration decreases by a factor of 3/175. Thus, Ni and either Th or Rb provide the greatest contrast in behaviour and are therefore the most useful for examining magmatic processes.

(b) On a log–log plot, all but two of the data points fall on a straight line, indicating that these are related by fractional crystallization. The most primitive magma is that with the lowest concentration of a highly incompatible element (in this case magma A), and because it falls on the fractionation trend can be considered the parental magma in this magma series.

(c) B and H fall above the fractionation trends on Figures A4 and A5. They are thus enriched in Ni compared with fractionated magmas, and so are likely to have formed by magma mixing. The end members that can account for both B and H must have compositions that fall on the intersection between the mixing trend and the fractionation trend. This is easily seen on the linear plot (Figure A5), as here the mixing line is a readily drawn straight line. The end members' compositions are thus estimated as 1.6 p.p.m. Th (11 p.p.m. Rb), 95 p.p.m. Ni and 11.1 p.p.m. Th (78 p.p.m. Rb), c. 4 p.p.m. Ni.

(d) The fractionated magmas would be expected to have phenocrysts that were in chemical and thermal equilibrium with their host groundmass. This would be indicated by straight crystal edges. The mixed magmas, however, would have inherited two populations of crystals, one from each end member. Each population would have been in chemical and thermal disequilibrium with the mixed magma, causing the crystals to undergo reactions with their host liquids. Crystals from the low temperature (evolved) magma would become corroded (and plagioclase would develop sieve textures, e.g. Figure 3.33). Crystals from the high temperature (primitive) magma would not dissolve, but, along with the corroded crystals, would eventually become overgrown by new mineral material that was in chemical and thermal equilibrium with the mixed magma. This would be seen in thin section as a thin continuous rim around the crystals (e.g. Figure 3.33).

(e) Sr does not change in composition, so
$Sr = Sr_o F^{D_{Sr} - 1}$
$300 = 300 F^{D_{Sr} - 1}$
$D_{Sr} = 1$

(the behaviour of Sr in these magmas follows the line labelled $D = 1$ in Figures 3.16 or A1). Table 3.4 shows that plagioclase is the only mineral with K_D for Sr that is greater than 1, olivine and augite have $K_D \ll 1$. If plagioclase was the sole fractionating phase, then D_{Sr} would equal 1.9, and Sr would be compatible and decrease with fractionation. For D_{Sr} to equal 1, there must be a mixture of plagioclase and olivine and/or augite in the fractionating assemblage. To find the proportion of plagioclase, we start with the definition of D (equation 3.6),

$$D_{Sr} = X_{plag} \times K_{Sr}^{plagioclase/liquid} + X_{augite} \times K_{Sr}^{augite/liquid} + X_{olivine} \times K_{Sr}^{olivine/liquid}$$

From Table 3.4, we make the simplifying approximation that

$K_{Sr}^{augite/liquid}$ and $K_{Sr}^{olivine/liquid} = 0$, to leave
$D_{Sr} = X_{plagioclase} \times K_{Sr}^{plagioclase/liquid}$
$1 = X_{plagioclase} \times 1.9$
$X_{plagioclase} = 1/1.9 = 0.53$

i.e. 53% of the fractionating assemblage is comprised of plagioclase.

Plagioclase fractionation leads to a negative europium anomaly, so we would expect to find such an anomaly in the highly fractionated magma represented by rock E.

SAQ 3.6 (a) True (see Section 3.1 and VC272: *Island Arc Magmatism: Santorini*)

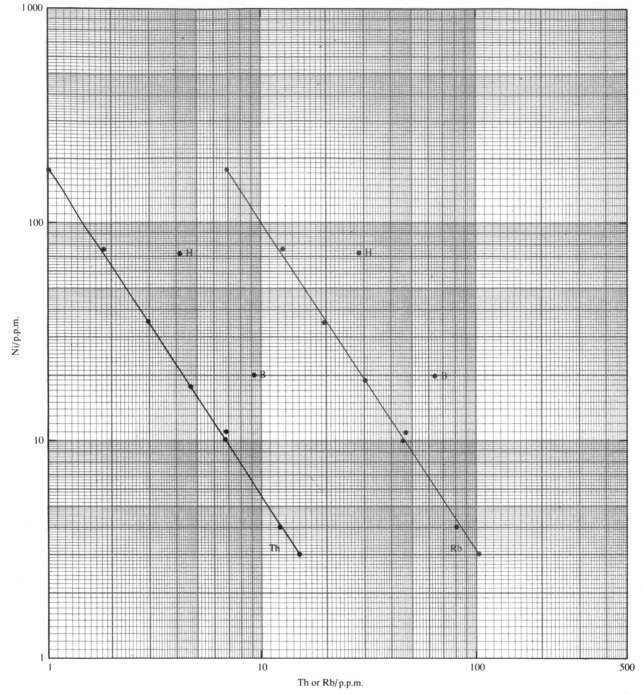

Figure A4 Completed log–log plots showing a straight line trend between Ni and Rb (red symbols and line) and the equally correct trend between Ni and Th (black symbols and line). Magmas H and B do not fall on the straight line trends.

(b) False. Field evidence shows Santorini to have been composed of at least four overlapping lava shields prior to the Minoan eruption (e.g. Figure 3.5).

(c) True. Craters on Nea Kameni and dykes in the northeastern caldera wall strike NE–SW and indicate magma passageways are aligned in that orientation.

(d) False. Discharge of hot mineral solutions from a hydrothermal system occur just below sea-level around the Kameni Islands.

SAQ 3.7 (a) The first major deposit was the ashfall layer which was dispersed by wind towards the east. This was followed by surge beds having wavy cross-stratification, and then the 'problematic beds' containing some very large lithic blocks of glassy lava. Finally, extensive ignimbrite sheets were emplaced and these now blanket much of Santorini.

(b) Dacite and andesite were erupted from a compositionally zoned magma chamber.

(c) The vent for the Minoan eruption is believed to have been between the present positions of Nea Kameni and the caldera wall near Thira. This position is indicated by the pattern of isopachs (lines of equal thickness of ash) of the Minoan ashfall layer which imply a maximum thickness for the ash at this location. That this marks the vent site is supported by additional evidence such as the proximity of the largest lithic blocks and their trajectories inferred from impact structures.

SAQ 3.8 (a) Fractional crystallization and magma mixing.

(b) Fractional crystallization is indicated by the many rocks plotting on reasonable straight line trends on log–log plots of a compatible trace element against an incompatible trace element. Magma mixing is implied by the presence of magmas that are relatively rich in compatible trace elements compared with those magmas previously identified as having formed by fractional crystallization. Petrographic examination confirms this through the presence of bimodal phenocryst populations inherited from

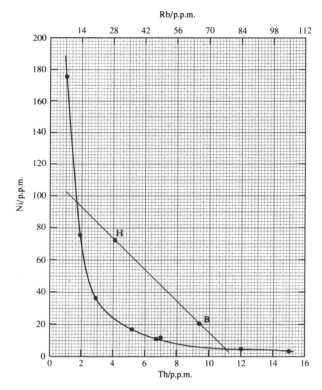

Figure A5 Completed plot, on linear paper, showing the curved trend of the fractionated magmas and the elevated Ni contents of magmas H and B. A straight line mixing trend through these points has been drawn.

two end-member magmas (e.g. coexisting augites with high and low Mg ratio cores overgrown by normal and reverse zoned rims) and signs of disequilibrium (sieve textured plagioclase). Banded pumices and lavas with variegated or blotchy-looking groundmasses also reveal the existence of different magmas being mixed together at the time of their eruption.

(c) The growth of crystals from a magma on the cool walls of a magma chamber releases fractionated liquid. The fractionated liquid has a different density (due to its different composition and, less importantly, lower temperature) from that of the still hot magma in the chamber interior. This density difference provides the fractionated liquid with buoyancy and it convects away from its site of origin. This separation of evolved liquid from the precipitated crystals under the influence of gravity is called convective fractionation. In calc-alkaline magmas, evolved magmas are lower in FeO_t than primitive magmas, so the fractionated liquids are relatively light and, therefore, float towards the chamber roof during convective fractionation. These evolved liquids pond beneath the roof of the magma chamber and so generate a zoned magma chamber in which fractionated liquids float on more primitive liquids.

SAQ 4.1 (a) False. Seismic studies have revealed crustal thicknesses of over 70 km in northern Chile (Figure 4.2 d).

(b) True. For example, active volcanoes are absent and the dip of the Benioff Zone is shallow in the vicinity of 30° S, where the Juan Fernandez Ridge is subducted (Figure 4.2 a and d).

(c) True. Turbulent flow ensures maximum heat exchange between the magma and the wall rocks. If the rocks have a low enough solidus, they will melt and contaminate the magma, resulting in a widening of the dyke (thermal erosion).

(d) False. Certain Andean volcanoes exhibit geochemical (variable ratios of $^{87}Sr/^{86}Sr$ and of highly incompatible trace elements) and field (disaggregated partially molten crustal xenoliths) evidence of crustal contamination. Such volcanoes include Cerro Galan and Lascar.

SAQ 4.2 The answers to this SAQ can be arranged in a table:

	Oceanic island arc	*Active continental margin*
range of SiO_2	basalt and basaltic andesites; more evolved magmas subordinate	andesites and dacites; more primitive and more evolved magmas are rare
tholeiitic or calc-alkaline	usually tholeiitic	usually calc-alkaline
volcanic landforms	composite cones	composite cones and calderas

SAQ 4.3 Silicic crust has high Rb/Sr. Over time, therefore, radioactive decay of ^{87}Rb to ^{87}Sr results in high $^{87}Sr/^{86}Sr$ in ancient silicic crust. This is in great contrast with the low $^{87}Sr/^{86}Sr$ of mantle-derived magmas that enter the crust. Magmas that have been contaminated by ancient silicic crust will have relatively high $^{87}Sr/^{86}Sr$. In contrast, young basic crust, with low Rb/Sr and hence low $^{87}Sr/^{86}Sr$, will hardly alter the $^{87}Sr/^{86}Sr$ of magma which it might contaminate.

SAQ 4.4 Fractional crystallization causes an increase in Rb/Sr but has no effect on $^{87}Sr/^{86}Sr$. This type of variation is shown by the series 1 magmas in Figure 4.15, and we conclude that fractional crystallization of a parent magma with $^{87}Sr/^{86}Sr = 0.704\,5$ has led to magma series 1. (Note that these magmas may also have experienced magma mixing — the $^{87}Sr/^{86}Sr$ ratios of the end members would have been the same and could not be any different when combined into a mixed magma.)

Series 2 show an orderly increase in $^{87}Sr/^{86}Sr$ with increasing Rb/Sr; the more evolved magmas have higher $^{87}Sr/^{86}Sr$. This is typical of magmas that have undergone progressive contamination by a high $^{87}Sr/^{86}Sr$ rock (such as ancient silicic crust) during fractional crystallization. This process of assimilation with fractional crystallization (AFC) is the most likely explanation for series 2.

Series 1 could have developed where the crust was thin and/or of young basic rock (a composition with a high solidus temperature and, therefore, not readily melted). Series 2 probably developed in thick ancient (high $^{87}Sr/^{86}Sr$) silicic (low solidus temperature and readily melted) crust. The Central Volcanic Zone of the Andes satisfy the above suggested requirements for series 2, while the other volcanic zones (Northern, Southern and Austral) are more appropriate for series 1 (Figure 4.2).

The evidence of crustal contamination in series 2 would be strengthened if the ratio of two highly incompatible trace elements (e.g. Rb/Th) changed with increasing Rb/Sr, as this would also reflect contamination by compositionally distinct (in terms of Rb/Th) crust. Constant Rb/Th in series 1 would indicate no contamination or contamination by rocks with the same Rb/Th as the parent magma (the same argument applies to the interpretation of the constant $^{87}Sr/^{86}Sr$ ratios). The presence of xenoliths with the appropriate Rb/Sr, Rb/Th and high $^{87}Sr/^{86}Sr$ ratios in series 2 magmas would also support the geochemical evidence for contamination; such xenoliths would not be expected in series 1 magma.

SAQ 5.1 (a) True (Section 5.1).

(b) False. They usually have at least several per cent normative anorthite, making them metaluminous (Table 5.1). Peralkaline granitoids are usually encountered in continental rift zones.

(c) False. Plutonic rocks share the chemical and mineralogical features of their contemporaneous volcanics; they are parts of the same magmatic system.

(d) True. This rate is based on estimates of excess crustal volume in arcs of known lifespan.

SAQ 5.2 There are three lines of evidence. (i) Igneous rocks at subduction zones are ultimately derived from partial melts that formed in the mantle wedge (Section 2). They thus represent mantle material that has been added to the crust. (ii) Geophysical studies reveal that arc crust is thicker than adjacent crust, which has been unaffected by subduction processes (e.g. Figures 4.1 and 5.8). The implication of this is that the crust has grown in volume in regions where it is influenced by subduction. (iii) Continental crust has grown by the incorporation of slivers of oceanic crust (ophiolite and displaced terranes).

SAQ 5.3 (a) Certain volcanic magmas have chemical compositions (such as high $^{87}Sr/^{86}Sr$ ratios) that show them to have assimilated pre-existing crust. Only a fraction of these magmas can be considered to be new additions to the crust.

(b) Most volcanic rocks at subduction zones have undergone a degree of crystal fractionation and have left cumulate crystals in the crust. Also, the existence of plutonic rocks in eroded arcs indicates that not all of the magma in subduction zones gets to the surface. The volume of volcanic rocks is thus likely to underestimate the total volume of magma.

SAQ 5.4 The docking age must be younger than the youngest pre-docking component of the terrane but older than the oldest intrusion that cuts the fault that transported the displaced terrane into its docking position. This method was used to estimate the docking age of the Amaime terrane in Colombia—see Section 5.3.2. Alternatively, the minimum docking age can be constrained by the oldest sedimentary cover derived from adjacent, post-docking, crust. This technique was used to date the docking of the Western Cordillera in Colombia (Section 5.3.2).

SAQ 5.5 Peruvian crust has grown only by the addition of magmas (Section 5.2), while that of Colombia has grown by both magmatism and the accretion of displaced terranes (Section 5.3.2).

Terrane accretion has occurred in Colombia because, at various times in the geological past, the Nazca Plate has approached the Colombian plate margin at a sufficiently oblique angle ($<25°$) for normal subduction to cease (extinguishing arc magmatism). This forced slivers of oceanic crust to be accreted onto the western margin of Colombia, extending the size of the South American Plate. In contrast, the Nazca Plate has always approached Peru more or less head on. So, in the absence of major transpression or strike–slip faulting, terranes have not been accreted to the Peruvian plate margin and only magmas have been emplaced into Peruvian crust (see Figure 5.7).

SAQ 6.1 (a) The Southern Uplands consists of Ordovician to Silurian ocean floor and trench sediments, in a structure similar to that found in modern accretionary prisms. The overall southward younging of the sequence implies a northward-directed destructive margin to the immediate south of the Southern Uplands. The Lower Ordovician mass flow deposits contain current structures that indicate transport from the northwest, but the granitic clasts within the conglomerates cannot be related to the geology currently to the northwest of the region. The implication is that the Southern Uplands has had (up until the Silurian) a separate geological history from the areas beyond either of its present margins. This satisfies the definition of a displaced terrane (see Block 1A, Section 3.3).

(b) Within the Caledonian–Appalachian orogenic belt, the area containing plutons of granite rocks most similar to those found as large boulders in certain Lower Ordovician conglomerates of the Southern Uplands is in northern Newfoundland. This implies that the Southern Uplands must have been located just south of Newfoundland during the Lower Ordovician in order to receive southerly transported granite clasts. To reach its present position in Scotland, the Southern Uplands must have been split from Newfoundland by sinistral displacement (cf. Figure 6.7).

SAQ 6.2 The collision date is bracketed by the youngest calc-alkaline magmas that were produced by subduction, and the oldest post- or syn-collision magmas that cut the suture. Subduction-related magmas south of the suture are essentially all Ordovician, but those north of the suture include examples that are as young as 408 Ma (Upper Silurian). The Cheviot granite and lavas (dated at 396 Ma) outcrop very close to the inferred position of the suture (Figure 6.2) and must have been emplaced at or after collision of the southern terrane(s) (e.g. Cadomia) with the Laurentian plate margin. Collision is thus bracketed between 408 and 396 Ma.

FURTHER READING

M. WILSON 1989 *Igneous Petrogenesis*. Unwin Hyman, London. pp. 466.

This textbook addresses the origin and nature of igneous rocks in the context of plate tectonic settings and processes. It covers the techniques of trace element and isotope geochemistry developed in Block 3. Island arcs and active continental margins are treated in separate chapters. While the book deals with many of the topics addressed in Block 3, this is an advanced textbook, and Wilson develops her treatment to more sophisticated levels than we have had time for.

K. G. COX, J. D. BELL AND R. J. PANKHURST, 1979 *The Interpretation of Igneous Rocks*. George Allen and Unwin Ltd, London. pp. 450.

This book has become a standard text on the techniques used to study igneous rocks and processes. It includes chapters on trace element and isotope geochemistry applied to fractional crystallization and contamination. Each chapter has student exercises with answers.

R. A. F. CAS AND J. V. WRIGHT, 1987 *Volcanic Successions Modern and Ancient*. Allen and Unwin, London. pp. 528.

This is a specialist textbook, but contains a useful chapter (chapter 15) on the relationships between volcanism and tectonic setting, and throughout the book frequent references are made to the volcanic products and processes found at particular arc volcanoes.

Field Guides

Examples of subduction-related rocks are to be found in many parts of the British Isles (Figure 6.2). We hope that you will be interested in seeing some of these rocks for yourself; the following is a selection of useful geological field guides and information.

D. A. ROBSON, 1976 *A Guide to the Geology of the Cheviot Hills*. Transactions of the Natural History Society of Northumbria, vol. 43, no. 1, pp. 23.

This provides a general description of the rocks and field relationships in this eroded volcano that lies on the Iapetus suture.

M. F. HOWELLS, B. E. LEVERIDGE AND A. J. REEDMAN, 1981 *Snowdonia*, George Allen and Unwin, Hemel Hempstead, Herts. pp. 119.

This provides an account of the geological background to, and field excusions in, the Lower Palaeozoic (including volcanic) rocks of Snowdonia.

B. ROBERTS, 1979 *The Geology of Snowdonia and Lleyn: An Outline and Field Guide*. Adam Hilger Ltd., Bristol, pp. 83.

This has a detailed outline of the geology of Snowdonia and Lleyn with detailed field excursion guides and a good geological map of the area.

F. MOSELEY, 1983 *The Volcanic Geology of the Lake District*. Macmillan, London, pp. 111.

This guide contains itineraries for excursions that feature a variety of Ordovician volcanics in the central Lake District, together with a short, but in places dated, introductory interpretation of the general geology of the region.

Loch Doon pluton

Much of this pluton, studied in the Home Kit exercise, lies on land operated by the Forestry Commission and is 'out of bounds'. However, the northeastern part of the pluton and its country rocks can be readily examined around the southwestern and southern shores of Loch Doon beside the unclassified Loch Doon Castle road. The intrusive contact is seen north of Cornish Loch. The plutonic rocks on the shore of Loch Doon are granodiorites. They locally contain abundant mafic inclusions of some interest and are cut by silicic dykes related to the pluton.

ACKNOWLEDGEMENTS

Critical comments on earlier drafts of this Block from Dr J. G. Fitton, University of Edinburgh, and Sir Malcolm Brown have helped enormously in the writing of the final text. Dr. J. P. P. Huijsmans is thanked for granting permission to use his geochemical data on Santorini rocks. Dr T. H. Druitt (University of Wales, Cardiff), Professor J. Keller (Freiburg University) and the Institute of Geology and Mineral Exploration, Athens, provided important details, information or help regarding the geology of Santorini. Grateful acknowledgement is also due to Dr A. G. Tindle (Open University) and the Forestry Commission for help in preparing the Loch Doon Home Kit. Thanks also go to Carol Whale, Pam Owen, Anita Chhabra, Janet Dryden and Marie-Claude Whitbourn for word processing drafts of this Block.

Grateful acknowledgement is made to the following sources for permission to use material in this Block:

Figure 2.2(a): H. Martin (1986) 'Effect of steeper Archean geothermal gradient on geochemistry of subduction-zone magmas', *Geology*, vol. 14, no. 9, p. 754, by permission of the author and the Geological Society of America, Inc.; *Figure 3.1*: M. Barton and J.P.P. Huijsmans (1986) 'Post-caldera dacites from the Santorini volcanic complex, Aegean Sea, Greece', *Contributions to Mineralogy and Petrology*, vol. 94, no. 4, p. 473, Springer-Verlag; *Figure 3.2*: T.H. Druitt, R.A. Mellors, D. Pyle and R.S.J. Sparks (1989) 'Explosive volcanism on Santorini, Greece', *Geological Magazine*, vol. 126, no. 2, p. 97, copyright © 1989 Cambridge University Press; *Figure 3.34*: J.P.P. Huijsmans and M. Barton (1989) 'Polybaric geochemical evolution of two shield volcanoes from Santorini, Aegean Sea, Greece', *Journal of Petrology*, vol. 30, no. 3, pp. 601 and 607, copyright © 1989 Oxford University Press; *Figure 4.1*: J.B. Gill (1981) *Orogenic Andesites and Plate Tectonics*, p. 48, Springer-Verlag; *Figure 4.2(a) and (c)*: A.M. Ziegler, S.F. Barrett and C.R. Scotes (1981) 'Palaeoclimate, sedimentation and continental accretion', *Philosophical Transactions of the Royal Society*, A301, p. 255, The Royal Society; *Figure 4.2(b)*: M. Barazangi and B.L. Isacks (1976) 'Spatial distribution of earthquakes and subduction . . .', *Geology*, November 1976, vol. 4, no. 11, p. 692, by permission of the authors and the Geological Society of America, Inc.; *Figure 4.2(d)*: R.S. Thorpe, P.W. Francis, M. Hamill and M.C.W. Baker 'The Andes', in R.S. Thorpe (ed.) (1982), *Andesites*, p. 189, copyright © 1982 John Wiley & Sons; *Figure 5.1(a)*: I.S.E. Carmichael, F.J. Turner and J. Verhoogen (1974) *Igneous Petrology*, p. 577, McGraw-Hill; *Figure 5.1(b)*: G.C. Brown, R.S. Thorpe and P.C. Webb (1984) 'The geochemical characteristics of granitoids in contrasting areas', *Journal of the Geological Society*, vol. 141, p. 416, the Geological Society, London; *Figure 5.3(a)*: S. Mahlburg Kay, R.W. Kay, H.K. Brueckner and J.L. Rubenstone (1983) 'Tholeiitic Aleutian arc plutonism: the Finger Bay pluton, Adak, Alaska', *Contributions to Mineralogy and Petrology*, vol. 82, p. 102, Springer-Verlag; *Figure 5.5*: G.F. Marriner and D. Millward (1984) 'The petrology and geochemistry of Cretaceous to Recent volcanism', *Journal of the Geological Society*, vol. 141, p. 474, the Geological Society, London; *Figure 5.6*: J.A. Aspden, W.J. McCourt and M. Brook (1987) 'Geometrical control of subduction-related magmatism . . .', *Journal of the Geological Society*, vol. 144, p. 896, by permission of the authors, the British Geological Survey and the Geological Society, London; *Figure 6.1*: N.J. Soper 'Timing and geometry of collision terrane accretion', in A.L. Harris and D.J. Fettes (eds) (1988) *The Caledonian–Appalachian Orogen*, no. 38, p. 482, the Geological Society, London; *Figures 6.3 and 6.4*: F. Mosely and D. Millward 'Ordovician volcanicity in the English Lake District', in D.S. Sutherland (ed.) (1982) *Igneous Rocks of the British Isles*, pp. 102 and 107, © 1982 John Wiley & Sons; *Figure 6.5*: C.J. Stillman and C.T. Williams (1978) 'Geochemistry and tectonic setting of some upper Ordovician . . .', in *Earth and Planetary Science Letters*, vol. 41, p. 303, Elsevier; *Figure 6.6*: W.E. Stephens and A.N. Halliday (1984) 'Geochemical contrast between late Caledonian granitoid plutons . . .', in *Transactions: Earth Sciences*, vol. 75, p. 267, by permission of the authors and the Royal Society of Edinburgh.